Janet Su

THE FREE STATE

A South African Response to
Chekhov's *The Cherry Orchard*

OBERON BOOKS
LONDON

WWW.OBERONBOOKS.COM

First published by Methuen in 2000

New edition published in 2011 by Oberon Books Ltd.
521 Caledonian Road, London N7 9RH
Tel: +44 (0.) 20 7607 3637/Fax: +44 (0.) 20 7607 3629
e-mail: info@oberonbooks.com
www.oberonbooks.com

A catalogue record for this book is available from the British
Library.

ISBN: 978-1-84943-133-0

Cover image by Design Advantage

Printed and bound by CPI Group (UK) Ltd, Croydon, CR0 4YY.

Introduction

It has to be said that transposing *The Cherry Orchard* to a South African setting is not a new notion: an expatriate friend of mine, Michael Picardie, wrote his version, *The Cape Orchard* published in 1987, which opened in October of that year in Plymouth and toured the UK, ending up at The Place in London. The playwright Ronald Harwood wrote a screenplay in 1992, which is wonderful, though as yet unmade. Barney Simon (late artistic director of the Market Theatre, Johannesburg, founded in 1976) first broached the idea to me in the late seventies. In repressive societies, certain classic plays take on a whole new meaning.

The three writers mentioned above are all South Africans and there are others from that country who have found inspiration in Chekhov – the playwright Reza de Wet, for one, springs to mind. The Afrikaner, especially, finds deep emotional affinities with the Russian passion for the land and its landscapes, for the size and remoteness of the estates, for the ebullient and sentimental people who inhabit them and, not least, for the complex symbiotic relationship between landowners and peasants. South Africa is a sad country and I think Russia is, too.

Having said that, the common ground stretches a little thinner, for whereas in Russia the common language between two estates is Russian, in South Africa there is no such binding unity, not in origin, nor history, nor culture. South Africa is polyglot and most South Africans will move from one language to another without noticing, even in a single phrase. Black South Africans have developed an urban lingo that melds many of the Nguni languages, rather like Italians getting the gist of Spanish. White South Africans, uneducated for the most part in black languages, nevertheless borrow what they need. (This is so common that in 1996, the OUP published its first *Dictionary of South African English*, all 810 pages of it, clarifying the genesis of countless expressions and words that I have used without thinking all my life.) A play is dialogue, not merely an interesting political thesis, and so a familiarity with the speech rhythms, the social nuances, the sense of humour, the complicated interplay between the races of such an ethnically vexed country is useful.

I don't suppose Chekhov's *Cherry Orchard* need necessarily be seen through the prism of politics – it is a great play and can be, therefore, all things to all men in all ages. But to a South African sensibility, where the very air you breathe is political, it becomes a play specifically about a new order taking over from the old. Lopakhin, a newly freed serf, at long last fulfils a dream by buying what had always been out of his reach, the estate of the neighbouring gentry. Such a possibility seemed impossibly remote in the Seventies, nor was it evident in the Eighties, even though by November 1985 tentative talks were starting in secret between Nelson Mandela and Kobie Coetzee. Barney Simon and I decided to put the idea on the back burner until the time for a new order arrived – if ever. It didn't look hopeful. In 1987, apartheid still in place, I directed *Othello* at The Market, using the racist metaphor of the play – the trashing of a potentially wonderful black/white love affair by a vengeful bigot – to do the work of highlighting the South African status quo.

By the end of the Eighties the world started changing more rapidly than anyone could have foreseen – glasnost, perestroika, the end of the Soviet empire and the consequent changes in the South African scenario. History had thrown up an unlikely pair of twins, Gorbachev and de Klerk, who would somehow see the writing on the wall and instigate remarkable change. In 1994 South Africa held its first elections – and on 30 June 1995 Barney Simon died. His heart gave out. It was shocking and it was tragic – he was far too young to die. He was a great man and had a profound influence on my thinking, as he did for many other people. 'An unnecessary death,' as Athol Fugard angrily put it at his graveside.

And so, perforce, there remained unfinished business to attend to for Barney. I was somehow determined to complete what we had first mooted together – *The Cherry Orchard* seen through South African eyes – and to play a latter-day Ranevskaya under his direction. He was a wonderful director; I would not easily have found a substitute for that particular collaboration. After his death, with the experience of transposing to a Johannesburg idiom Brecht's *Good Woman of Setzuan*, I felt that the more subtle, more indefinable play might now be within my grasp. A silly

Janet Suzman as Lucy Rademeyer in *Free State*
© Stephen Vaughan

cartoon above my desk – of the half-swallowed frog desperately throttling the pelican, with the legend: 'Don't *ever* give up' – I eventually replaced with my favourite Barney Simon aperçue: 'People don't know what they don't know.' It had become increasingly obvious to me that rethinking Chekhov begged more for a touch of visceral flair than mere dogged application.

There are certain unavoidable imperatives the moment you consider the implications of setting Chekhov's play in contemporary South Africa. The most obvious, as I have said, is the overall thrust of the play: a farmer, Lopakhin, newly empowered by his money and his liberty, buys the estate of his once rich, now impoverished neighbours. His father, a serf, had once been owned by the Ranevskys, but The Freedom allows the son to forgive the family. Lopakhin's evident love for the owner of the estate, Liubov Andreevna, stems, it seems, from unnamed acts of help and kindness by her to him. The South African take on it makes no sense at all, therefore, unless the character becomes a black man.

But who? Rich he must be, but how? How exactly did he get rich? In the original, Lopakhin has made his money from several thousand acres of poppies which sold well. In South Africa the likelihood of a rich farmer being black is remote, and even less a rich black *neighbouring* farmer. The Group Areas Act saw to that. So the representative of the new order pointed to a member of the black entrepreneurial class now establishing itself in South Africa – a Cyril Ramaphosa, an Nthato Motlana who, having mastered the capitalist ethic so brilliantly, can now afford to restore lost dignity and play the whites at their own game. The new character, Leko Lebaka, began to take shape.

But how is the relationship of affection and even admiration that he holds for the family to be explored? Why does he try so hard to persuade them to save themselves by proposing they lease out their land for summer dachas, before finally buying the land for himself? Is he reluctant to appear greedy? Does he genuinely want them to find their own way out of the mess they're in? Is he in love with Lulu? Such relationships are rare in South Africa. One solution appeared to reside in those liberal-minded whites who helped their staff up the educational ladder. White

6

landowners of a decent turn of mind frequently started little schools for the children of their workers. In cities, whites would salve their consciences by paying for the education of servants and their children. It was an intrinsic part of white paternalism.

Say this family of ours had seen to the education of the young man, Leko, (whose father worked for them) and finding him an apt pupil, eventually sent him off to do a post-graduate MBA? Say the young man turned out to be a highly successful businessman, always made welcome in the family whenever he returned for a visit? There is nothing more gratifying than a successful investment in someone's potential.

But another dimension was necessary: friendship, not mere gratitude. The nature of the household itself needed to play a part – an open house, holding its arms wide to all comers. Gaev, in the original, makes an emotional speech in Act One to the bookcase and its contents. That bookcase, it seemed to me, should come into its own, achieving a real importance to the people who had used it over the years. That bookcase should provide a window on to an otherwise closed world to those who were encouraged to share in its treasures – philosophy, history, law, politics. To those deprived of such things, the disenfranchised, its books would be a source of learning and revelation. The single bookcase thus expands its importance to become a virtual library in this version.

And what sort of family would insist on an open house? Fearless liberal-minded folk, most likely, who found the existing status quo anathema and, although liberals have gone into history now, trailing clouds of opprobrium, they had their uses. An informing spirit was needed. Who? I've always loved Chekhov's offstage characters – like Protopopov in *Three Sisters*. The dead husband seemed ripe for a history. All we know about him in the original, via his widow Liubov Andreevna, is that he was always in debt and died of too much champagne. It is the prerogative of genius not to explain too much.

But mere adaptors need to justify every thought. I wanted to include the Afrikaners into the dramatic equation; a South African play would be irretrievably diminished without that overriding presence. Lest anyone should assume that the Afrikaner was all bad, I was keen to give the decent ones airtime. André Brink,

Jack Klaff as Leo Guyver in *Free State*
© Stephen Vaughan

Jeffery Kissoon as Alexander in *Free State*
© Stephen Vaughan

Breyten Breytenbach, J.M. Coetzee, Athol Fugard (albeit half-Irish) are household names in the world of letters. And then there's Elsa Joubert, Menan du Plessis, Antjie Krog, Eugene Marais, Karel Schoeman – and legions more. Although dissident elements in South Africa – Jewish, Gentile, Indian – were all too evident, it should be recalled that it was a distinctly Afrikaans group of unhappy intellectuals who gathered together and travelled to Lusaka at the end of the Eighties to speak to the ANC in exile.

The greatest Afrikaans political dissident of all was Bram Fischer, who in 1964 led the defence of Nelson Mandela in the Rivonia Trial and in 1966 was sentenced to life imprisonment, where he died nine years later. I wanted his legacy to live in the play, and so I turned the dead husband into an Afrikaans lawyer working for the Struggle, who would die of drink and grief before seeing his dreams of a democratic South Africa realised. It is his liberating spirit that presides over the house, his portrait hangs in the nursery and his widow, who loved him deeply, has willingly imbibed his liberality and embodies his continuing ethos. Chekhov's Liubov Andreevna Ranevskaya (Liuba means love) thus take on a more politically adventurous hue in her South African sister, Lulu Rademeyer.

Such a couple would have had a lasting influence on the young Leko, not least because they would have been the first white people of his acquaintance to speak to him as an equal. When Leko and Lulu first meet and she solves his problems in a trice – with such ease and grace ('she gave my father a job straight off') – the impressionable lad of fifteen might have been open to an instant crush on his young saviour.

This scenario seemed to answer some of the requirements of the new setting, and would, I hoped, provide the grounds for an atmosphere in which frank talk could take place. Most especially in Act Two, the races need to express their personal parameters, politically, socially. However implausible, I was damned if the exploration of personal affection and friendship between black and white should not be broached. There is more than enough dramatic exploitation of animosity between the races, and anyway there are more good people in South Africa than not good. Chekhov's healing spirit needed an outlet, and Mandela's new democracy seemed the apt place to celebrate such things.

The ground laid thus for free and frank discussion, in what exact moment in history could such encounters believably occur? The action, to obey the seasonal aspect of Chekhov's play must start in the spring and move towards autumn. That dictated the September after the first April elections, when the cherry blossoms would be at their full beauty and the optimism of the elections would still be in the air. A window of time of six months, not yet dissipated by the carping and questioning that the ensuing years inevitably brought, would cover the journey of the play.

Real revolutions, however, take longer than that. As Barney Simon had said: 'Freedom through legislation has come suddenly and swiftly, and that is cause for great celebration. But freedom of the heart and mind is lagging far behind. We struggle every day to *realise* the difference between what was and what is.' Chekhov's pre-revolutionary Russians also struggled in contradiction and confusion, dreaming of better times. Our better times had come and yet on the surface nothing had changed. The political satirist, Pieter Dirk Uys, tells the story of an angry young black man at a political rally shouting out: 'We fought for freedom and look what we got – democracy!'

The central metaphor of the cherry orchard itself became an intriguing symbol: its abundant blossoms speaking of generations of careful husbandry and the family's sentimental attachment to that springtime effulgence speaking of beauty for beauty's sake – a very 'white' indulgence. But the point is that the cherry orchard has ceased to bear fruit; it is played out and, what is more the bottom has dropped out of the cherry market. The glorious white blossoms are only a nostalgic memory of what was once pleasingly profitable to just one small family – a perfect image for the dying throes of apartheid. It's worth recalling that apartheid, besides being most abominable, was the most unaffordable political credo ever devised in a time of peace.

Where, geographically, should the play be set? The Cape obviously deserved consideration, where old historic estates proliferate and where people of English extraction have lived, some in splendour, for centuries. But to swop the cherry orchard for a vineyard would diminish not only the iconography but also bring into question the business failure of the estate; the wine industry remains pretty healthy. Most crucially, the rural ethnic mix in the Cape is predominantly Coloured, which would imbalance the black/white thesis.

The only area of South Africa where the weather is right for growing cherries is in the eastern Free State, hence a cherry festival held every year in the little town of Ficksburg on the northern Lesotho border. The Free State is a province thought by most people, South Africans included, to be exclusively settled by Afrikaners. Not so. After the Basotho Wars, English people were encouraged to buy land along the border at knock-down prices to provide a buffer between the British Protectorate, the little Kingdom of Lesotho, and the troublesome Boers of the Orange Free State Republic. These areas, bought largely by people of English extraction, are known colloquially as 'rooi-kolle' – literally 'red-collar' (redneck) districts. The settlers kept themselves aloof from the local Afrikaans farmers for reasons of language and heritage as much as snobbery. Areas round Thaba Nchu, Westminster (named after the Dukes of Westminster who acquired enormous areas of land), Clocolan and, extending up to Viljoenskroon, Ficksburg and beyond, are still settled by about twenty-five percent English speakers. Many of them were fortune-hunters who made their wealth in 1860s and 1870s in the Kimberley diamond rush, bought shares in De Beers Consolidated and fathered the dynasties of new land-rich farmers.

My mind was made up when I came across the history of one great house in particular, 'Prynnsberg', near Clocolan. The house, a marvellous stone mishmash of architectural oddities, still stands under its rocky krans looking out over a stunning landscape that stretches to the distant range of the Maluti mountains on the Lesotho border. The Newberrys had bought it from Prynn (who had fought in the Basotho Wars) in 1879 and for four generations it shone as a grand country rendezvous, famous for its buckshoots – herds of imported bles-bok – and grand house parties. Over the years it had been extravagantly furnished in neo-Egyptian style and remained untouched until the contents – a time warp of the Victorian era – were sold off by Sotheby's SA in 1996, the biggest ever sale of its kind in South Africa.

The estate had come free of entailment with the last heir, Trevor Newberry, but he died suddenly of cirrhosis at the age of forty-nine having drunk most of his money away, and, worse, he died intestate. He had been a reclusive bachelor (shades of Chekhov's Gaev), frightened of fortune hunters and quite unable to recoup his lost fortune. Female profligacy had brought the once fabulous fortune to its knees. I had found my local exemplar of Chekhov's landed bourgeoisie.

The children of that marriage between Lulu and Johan Rademeyer (for that became the dead husband's name) are Anna and a little son who, at only seven, was drowned; not a shock any mother could bear. There is another daughter, Maria (Varya in the original). Once again, Chekhov is vague about Varya's provenance – we merely learn that she is of 'simple origin' and probably adopted. Michael Frayn, in the introduction to his version of the play, proposes the notion that Varya could well be the result of the dead husband's philanderings, hence her ready absorption as a member of the family. Such *droit de seigneur* has been an habitual pastime with Afrikaners for a good three centuries, hence the Cape Coloured people. Johan, for all his liberal beliefs, would not have been above a youthful fling with a maid, so the idea of Maria (Varya) being his love-child seemed feasible. The abandonment of the baby by her mother is very unAfrican, though, and more difficult to accept, but I had to imagine a very young mother who took fright and ran away after the birth.

It is true to say, however, that such an adoption in the excessively conservative Free State would be rare, and would excite terrific prejudice from the locals, but I do know of one Afrikaans family in particular, who made a point of adopting black children; South Africa was always rich in anomalies. Since this play deals with the exceptions rather than the rules, however, I considered Frayn's excellent idea of a love-child in this more complicated context workable.

It gave me some pleasure to be able to pack Maria off to the Cape at the end of the play, where her own people truly have their home. Courageous Maria, always a little on the outside, but realising in the end that she must learn to stand on her own two feet and make her own life. Just so were the Cape Coloured people neither quite here nor quite there in the past history of South Africa.

As to her half-sister, Anna, Chekhov has her a year younger and only on the brink of life. But she needs to be politically aware in this modern version and filled with the excitement of a new young South African – a first time voter. She represents, with such a father, the perfect amalgam for the new democracy, the blood of both white races coursing in her veins, and eager to sit at the feet of her black lover and imbibe his ideas. So here she is over eighteen, already at university in Johannesburg and ripe to discard the anachronistic lifestyle that has nurtured her. Her father's influence is strong. There have always been cross-colour affairs (cf. Fugard's *Statements after an Arrest under The Immorality Act*) but whereas in the old regime the excitement of secrecy gave a certain frisson, they can now operate with an openness that permits a true meeting of minds to prevail over mere passion (Chekhov's tutor is at pains to declare he is 'far removed from such banality') – which is not to exclude entirely the thrill of entering unknown territory.

The tutor, Piotr Trofimov – now named Pitso Thekiso – here has exciting room for development. He becomes the opposing spirit to the self-made pragmatic capitalist, the rags-to-riches entrepreneur, Leko Lebaka. Pitso is the idealistic activist, impatient with the rate of change and fearful that market forces will undermine the socialist revolutionary flame that lit the fires of grass-roots opposition (roughly PAC v. ANC). He too was born on the estate, educated by the family, became interested in Johan's work with legal aid, was funded at Fort Hare University by the family to read law, interrupted his studies to join the freedom movement and was sent by the ANC for training in Russia before returning home to be an underground activist.

The thirteen-year-old Anna, who once followed Pitso about the estate as he played with the little son, Gerrit, he finds now, on his return, to be less of the kid sister he'd known most of his life and more a desirable young woman. Anna and Pitso thus represent a sort of ideal, however unrealistic – the possibility of cross-racial harmony in an integrated modern South Africa. I am particularly fond of the fact that, having learnt Russian, his little love poem to Anna at the end of Act One can be Chekhov's original. In any case little poems in praise of flowers or sunshine (praising sunshine in Africa?) in the Nguni languages are, to my knowledge, non-existent, so this is a happy flourish. I also took some delight in tracing Piotr's obsession with his lost galoshes – objects quite incomprehensible to South Africans. So the galoshes are replaced by a Russian fur hat – a love token from a certain amorous young Muscovite called...Varya, and my excuse to doff my own hat to the Master. Footwear became equally interesting, Yepikhodov's squeaky boots turning into worn-out trainers. (Boots are for white boys, especially hated military white boys.)

In defining the seemingly opposing views taken by Pitso and Leko, it was vital that Leko should also have a history of activity in the Struggle, although his life during those years is more shrouded than Pitso's. I first imagined that Leko himself was a serving member in the ANC executive and that he knew all about Pitso's secondment overseas – indeed had monitored his progress – but in the end that seemed a trifle too pat. So now Leko briefly reveals an intriguing history of incarceration and torture, reluctantly showing Pitso a damaged hand. This also acknowledges Lopakhin's uncontrollable hands. The two men can thus have a legitimate reconciliation, Leko having finally admitted his political bona fides.

Leko's lack of a wife is, however, thoroughly unAfrican and I needed to justify this particular solitariness, if only to myself, by having him unsettled in some way by his long-standing and ever unresolved relationship with Lulu. While Leko's fortunes prospered, those of the estate dwindled – Leo's bad management and Lulu's profligacy – until by the time the story begins, bankruptcy beckons. Leko does all he can to devise profitable schemes to save the estate from ruin, and protect his beloved, maddening Lulu. When these attempts prove hopeless and the estate comes up for auction, Leko takes the plunge and bids for it.

Thus, with the flick of a finger, Leko becomes the owner of Lulu's patrimony – a dubious triumph; their relationship is forever changed by this act. The family is broken apart and follows its separate ways. Lulu will return to her old lover in

Dorothy Gould as Karlotta in *Free State*
© Stephen Vaughan

Paris, conscious that the five generations of her family lived on borrowed time; Leko is aware that although the world is his as it never could be in the bad old days, something is gone from it forever. For both, in some ways, a burden is lifted. That their colour and history predicates an eventual separation, while more realistic, is sad. Leko has both lost and won; Lulu too. It is a bitter-sweet realisation. But Lulu, at the last, has the courage to thank her friend for setting her free. The burden of living with apartheid has been lifted from her shoulders.

In bidding for the cherry orchard, Leko also fulfils a secret, if unspoken ambition. Long ago, the Sotho peoples had occupied these lands. An additional resonance, in this version, can thus enter the lists – the restoration of Leko's ancient tribal lands. It is not possible to consider the implications of settler lands in South Africa without pondering this question; the Land Restitution Commission is one of the busiest quangos in the country and the vexed question of not only 'black-spot' forced removals, but the unequal distribution of rich farming land is ignored at your peril. One wonders if the same thought might have lurked in the back of the kulak Lopakhin's mind too?

This unstated fascination Leko has for Lulu, beginning in adolescence and subverted by the busy years in between, also partly explains why he cannot bring himself to propose to Maria. In the original it seems a foregone conclusion that the two will marry, and only Lopakhin's crippling shyness prevents him going down on his knees. Here, however, this is not a given, and these other strands of colour and amorous obsession duly influence the outcome of the proposal scene. Luckily Maria, like the little maid, Kele, is a modern young woman and marriage is not the be-all and end-all of life for either of them. The two girls in the original are products of their time, poor things, and are far more stricken.

Leo Guyver (Leonid Gaev) – Lulu's elder brother – is a man who has never grown up. Coddled by his protective mother, nannied by his manservant, indulged by his sister, born to indolence and wealth, he is no less than a big baby. He is fifty-one in Chekhov, though seems older; I add ten years to adjust his lifespan to South African events, but he seems younger. He takes refuge in billiards, is prey to sentimental speechifying, can't face the realities, has never left home and is a bit of a snob, though his heart is a good one. Certainly he has never embraced the hard-nosed responsibilities incumbent upon the scion of a great house. He veers between trying hard to embrace the new thinking and immensely disliking the whole set-up – a common liberal dilemma. Like everyone else in the story, he adores his sister who makes him feel more alive, but will in the end be abandoned by her. He is basically harmless and out of his time – the epitome of someone born to a position he can no longer even try to justify: the white man in Africa.

I gave up on the question of language, because of course in reality Leko and Pitso would converse together in Sotho. I partly solved it with the other black characters by having the 'valet', Nyatso, arrogantly declare that he refuses to speak anything but English now, thus forcing Kele and Khokoloho to speak English as well. Nyatso becomes an interesting personification of those exiles who return and cannot adjust. He has learned certain skills and imbibed a certain lifestyle in the ambiance of Paris and can no longer 'go back'. In essence he is probably more in love with himself than with anyone else. This presumed cold-heartedness arose from the original, where Yasha is horribly uncaring about his mother coming to visit him; again very unAfrican. Nyatso is a young man who has lost his most basic African values and I fear for him in the future. In his favour, he suffers from the realisation that he has grown out of his roots, but cannot unlearn what he has learned. He is also very uncaring about Kele's crush on him, but he gets his come-uppance for treating the young girl so cavalierly; in this version she slaps his face for him, something that put-upon Dounyasha in the original could never have done. Rather like Phoebe in *As You Like It*, Kele realises the virtues of faithfulness embodied by patient, peaceable Khokoloho. The newly independent young woman, who so confuses old Putswa, has her triumphant moment.

And as to Khokoloho, (Yepikhodov in the original) – he was very difficult to Africanise. A sentimental romantic with suicidal tendencies and literary pretensions, endemically clumsy, fatalistic, maudlin, poetical, introspective – very Slavic, very Chekhov. In the original he has a nickname – literally 'Twenty-

17

two Misfortunes' – which I'm sure is funny in Russian. The Sotho nickname I found for him – Parathlathlé – if not instantly amusing to the English ear, at least has the value of authenticity. It's also impossible to translate, but 'a loose cannon-ball' will do. He is a young man who has given his heart to Kele and gradually learns that devotion is not always rewarded. He is a thoughtful and honest individual – possibly the norm among his peers, who never got further than Standard Five at school. Not everyone can be prodigiously talented. Yepikhodov mentions reading Buckle, whoever he may be, so I have Khokoloho looking for guidance from the Bible – shades of a missionary schooling and a spiritual bent.

We are also conscious of a growing political awareness in Khokoloho – the new South Africa is going to be his oyster and he knows it. Leo is training him up to take over the management of the farm and Leko confirms that trust at the end by employing him as just that. In Act Three, when Leko buys the estate, it is he who begins singing the famous protest song 'Shosholoza', turning it into the song of triumph it has become. And when the family breaks up, secure of employment by his new black master, he cannot hide his delight; his pride revels in the new dignity conferred on his people. I should add that I'm not at all sure that he will have Kele back after the way she's treated him, older and wiser though they both surely are by the end.

Karlotta, the family clown, a mysterious cucumber-eating German with a circus background in the original, is as much a member of the household as the other adoptees. Her sole German phrase in the Chekhov, *Guter mensch aber schlechter Musikant*, is so temptingly near to the Afrikaans (*Goeie mens maar 'n slegte musikant)* that I found no necessity to retain her original nationality. In any case, no English-speaking family would have employed a German as a governess.

A foundling brought up in an orphanage, though unlikely in Afrikaans society where some distant relative would most likely have taken her in, was the only way to account for Karlotta's solitary state. Some poor little pregnant white girl abandoning her unwanted baby in panic can't only be the norm in big cities; Bloemfontein is quite big enough for that too. I've not ignored her circus heritage, as Chekhov's idea is just too good to shake off, but instead of having her run away from the orphanage to join the big-top in an earlier effort, she just dreams of it. She's trained as a kindergarten teacher and is eventually recruited as his secretary by Rademeyer, to whom she is devoted. After his death, she takes on the housekeeping, looking after the two girls when Lulu flees to Europe after the death of her son, until Maria takes over the reins. By osmosis Karlotta simply becomes a fixture and a fitting – the maddest element in a fairly bohemian household. At the end, she is perhaps the saddest, having nowhere to go, but without an ounce of self-pity. In having her address her ID card at the beginning of Act Two, I was keen to highlight the whole issue of identity in South Africa, and most particularly that of the Afrikaner today. She could be seen as the lonely representative of a sidelined people, betraying the sort of dotty self-absorption that led her tribe, the Afrikaners, up the wrong historical alley. Her begging for a job from a black man is a poetic irony that will, I hope, not be lost on us.

B. S. Pickett (Boris Semyonov Pischik) is an old-regime relic too. A kindly old redneck farmer, often sozzled for lack of a wife, his land lies adjacent to the Guyvers'. He is continually fazed by his daughter Daphne (Dashenka, another favourite off-stage character) and her advanced ideas. He finds Lulu a dazzling exotic and is a frequent visitor to the house, no doubt to relieve the boredom of his existence. Like Leo, he is hopeless at farm management, and prey to the droughts that so often afflict the Free State farmer, and is shameless about borrowing money to tide him over. In the original, a white (china?) clay is found in his land by some prospecting Englishmen, restoring his modest fortunes. Here a more contemporary find seemed desirable and I was pleased to discover that molybdenum (a chemical element that gives strength to alloys; used especially for space exploration) exists in the Free State. Such a find would certainly excite a British mining company, so I could retain Chekhov's prospecting Englishmen. Somehow one knows that the poor chap would have been taken for a ride. His nickname, 'Pik', means 'little' in Afrikaans, so I imagine he's a large shambling sort of a fellow. He affects to fall for Karlotta and they both know it's nonsense.

The advent of the Stranger in Act Two speaks for itself: he is the embodiment of the millions 'out there', as yet untouched by any material benefits of the revolution. Russia's unholy vagrant transmutes into one of Africa's predatory, glimmering survivors.

The histories of these characters began to represent most sections of South African society and more crucially enabled a slant towards colour rather than status or class. I find productions set in an English context often slant towards the latter. The matter of colour cannot be sidestepped in a story set in South Africa – it infects everything we think and do – so the original play perforce takes on a dimension which Chekhov's pure white feudal system cannot address. An example: Chekhov's servants are always happily in and out of their masters' houses. He exposes the snobbery of people who are not used to this easy familiarity in the horrifically embarrassing scene in *Three Sisters*, where the arriviste Natasha berates the old servant for not getting up in her presence. I have experienced such rudeness with newly arrived immigrants. But in this case, where living with servants is the norm, a bantering, easygoing manner is more usual. The subtler social complications of black visitors to a white house, however, had to be more delicately monitored in order to be believable in a South African context.

As the play in its new setting started to reveal itself, I found that the generational gap between the characters began to open ever wider. In general, the difficulty in adapting to a free society is in direct proportion to the age of the individual. The young ones – Kele, Pitso, Anna, Maria, Khokoloho – with differing degrees of awareness, are all ready and willing to embrace the new dispensation and go with the flow. The older people, on the other hand – Leo, Putswa, Karlotta, Pik – while doing their damnedest to adjust themselves to a new mindset, yet retain a certain cynicism that in other parts of the world might be seen as politically incorrect, but in South Africa is current vocabulary. Lulu I like to think of as colour-blind and free of prejudice – the type that sees 'Othello's visage in his mind'.

Thus Putswa, the ancient manservant, clings to the old certainties of the master-servant relationship. One of the few exchanges that didn't ask to be altered was in Act Two when

Chekhov has Firs refer to The Freedom (of the Serfs) with disdain. There are certain pragmatic old parties in South Africa too, who daren't admit it, but feel a distinct nostalgia for the clearer upstairs-downstairs delineations of yore. Devoted to Leo – and in the same boat as regards radical change in the status quo – Putswa is an unrepentant member of the old guard, a veritable old gentleman. At the end he is left behind – unintentionally forgotten – eventually to fade away, one must assume. That, in the new South Africa, speaks for itself.

This resistance to change turns things upside down, in that the younger members of the story seem more mature than their elders. Lulu and Leo appear almost childishly irresponsible in their disinclination to face the realities of imminent bankruptcy. It is tempting to draw a parallel: in refusing to recognise the danger they are in, and therefore doing nothing to prevent it, both Lulu and Leo represent the attitude of many decent-minded folk who, by doing nothing about apartheid, condoned it.

Among the hundreds of details that needed reinterpretation, Lopakhin's endearing resort to a misquoted bit of *Hamlet* in Act Two demanded a radical rethink. I can't imagine anything less likely than a black businessman attempting a proposal in blank verse; Thabo Mbeki's fondness for quoting Shakespeare is unusual to say the least. I could always have cut it, but it's a stroke of genius on Chekhov's part and I was keen to try to realise its comic potential. Thus *Hamlet* had to be a part of his shared history with Lulu and to be introduced early on in the play so that his surprising resort to (mis)quoting from it in Act Two could be organically justified. I hope I've done just that.

I began to see, as South Africa dictated its own mad logic, that the characters, though recognisable, are emphatically not stereotypical. Anyway, Chekhov is far too original a playwright to encourage banality and, since Mandela himself is such an exceptional person, I hope this might prove acceptable in the South African context. Although every decision on the characters and their history is based on fact, while retaining the dynamics and, as far as possible, the intentions of the original, it is well to remember that this is, after all, but a play. Indeed, I came to think, as I wrote it, that these invented South Africans are probably nearer in nature to Chekhov's Russians, if lacking a certain spirituality, than the English sometimes fancy they are: ebullient, emotional, unsophisticated, blunt, hospitable, hard-drinking, sometimes brutal, and living in cloud-cuckoo land. The sale of the cherry orchard brings that delusion to an end.

Janet Suzman
August 2011

Esmeralda Bihl as Maria and Janet Suzman in *Free State*
© Stephen Vaughan

The production of a previous South African *Cherry Orchard* was performed at the Birmingham Repertory Theatre from 23 May to 14 June 1997 with the following cast:

LUCY RADEMEYER *Estelle Kohler*

LEO GUYVER *Jack Klaff*

MARIA *Esmeralda Bihl*

ANNA *Patricia Boyer*

PUTSWA *Allister Bain*

NYATSO *Joseph Jones*

DIKELEDI *Moshidi Motshegwa*

KHOKOLOHO *Sello Motloung*

KARLOTTA *Dorothy Gould*

MASOPHA LEBAKA *Burt Caesar*

PITSO THEKISO *Fana Mokoena*

SIMON PICKFORD *Peter Cartwright*

Directed by Janet Suzman

Designed by Johan Engels

Lighting by Tim Mitchell

Music by Didi Kriel

The Birmingham Play was written by Janet Suzman based on the translation by Tania Alexander. Acknowledgements to Roger Martin's original 'South Africa' adaptation.

The Free State was written in 1999.

Fifth Amendment, Birmingham Repertory Theatre
and the West Yorkshire Playhouse present

BARCLAYS Stage

Partners with THE ARTS COUNCIL OF ENGLAND

THE
FREE
STATE

A South African
response to Chekhov's
The Cherry Orchard

STARRING

JANET SUZMAN
JEFFERY KISSOON
JACK KLAFF

Darlington
Civic Theatre

DARLINGTON
BOROUGH COUNCIL

Tuesday 29 February -
Saturday 4 March 2000

In 2000 *The Free State* was performed with Janet Suzman playing Lucy Rademeyer & co-directed by her and Martin Platt.

ALEXANDER MASOPHA LEBAKA (LEKO) *Jeffery Kissoon*

DIKELEDI (KELE) *Marva Alexander*

KHOKOLOHO *Sello Motloung*

PUTSWA *Larrington Walker*

ANNA *Patricia Boyer*

MARIA *Esmeralda Bihl*

LUCY RADEMEYER (LULU) *Janet Suzman*

LEO GUYVER *Jack Klaff*

B.S. PICKETT (PIK) *Peter Cartwright*

NYATSO *Lebohang Elephant*

KARLOTTA *Dorothy Gould*

PITSO THEKISO (PIET) *James Ngcobo*

Directed by Janet Suzman with Martin L Platt

Designed by Johan Engels

Music by Didi Kriel

Lighting Design by Tim Mitchell

The Free State is set in 1994.

This play is dedicated to Nelson Mandela in celebration of the arrival of the new order in a democratic South Africa.

Produced by UK Arts International.

This production toured to

Birmingham Repertory Theatre: 18 Feb – 26 Feb
Darlington Civic Centre: 29 Feb – 4 Mar
Bath Theatre Royal: 7 March – 11 Mar
Poole Arts Centre: 14-18 Mar
West Yorkshire Playhouse: 21 Mar – 1 Apr
Richmond Theatre: 3 Apr – 8 Apr

This play is dedicated to

Nelson Rolihlahla Mandela

Characters

THE HOUSEHOLD

LUCY RADEMEYER (LULU)
mistress of the estate, a widow; fifties.

LEO GUYVER
her brother the owner; a bachelor; sixty.

MARIA
Lucy's late husband's child, adopted by her;
twenty-three.

ANNA
Lucy's daughter; eighteen.

PUTSWA
the ancient manservant; eighties.

NYATSO
Lucy's 'valet'; twenties.

DIKELEDI (KELE)
the housemaid; seventeen.

KHOKOLOHO
trainee manager of the estate; late twenties.

KARLOTTA
the Afrikaans secretary, now retired;
sixties to seventies.

THE FRIENDS

ALEXANDER MASOPHA LEBAKA (LEKO)
an entrepreneur; forties to fifties.

PITSO THEKISO (PIET)
a radical student; late twenties to thirties.

B. S. PICKETT (PIK)
a neighbouring farmer; sixties and upwards.

THE STRANGER
any age.

In Sotho, the name Putswa means 'greybeard', Nyatso means 'snob', and Khokoloho means, roughly, 'a loose cannon-ball'. In Afrikaans, Pik means 'small', Klippie means 'stone'.

SETTING

The place: the Clocolan area of the Free State.

The time: September 1994, six months after the first democratic elections.

Act 1: September (Spring)

Act 2: January (Summer)

Act 3: February 22nd

Act 4: March (Autumn)

Act One

Early September – spring – about 4.30 a.m.

A large high-ceilinged room. Two huge free-standing bookcases flank either side of a large central window, closed with wooden shutters. The shelves are packed with books (unmistakably legal volumes in one bookcase, in the other children's books, novels, biography, politics, history, drama, etc. and family bric-á-brac like old wooden tennis racquets, cricket bats, a small TV set, photo albums, etc).

A yellow-wood floor with rich old rugs. Framed family photographs on the walls. A large oil portrait of a man standing propped in front of the legal bookcase: Johan Rademeyer.

SR: A door leads to ANNA's room; SL: another to the rest of the house. Centrally – a comfortable sofa and coffee-table. DSC a child-sized table set with three baby chairs. On one of them sits a very worn teddy bear. SR: a high-backed wing chair; SL: a desk with a lamp and a chair.

A dark dawn is just visible through the slats of the closed shutters.

LEKO, asleep in the wing chair, is lit by the warm glow of a bar heater next to him and the flicker of a soundless TV in front of him. His regular snores gently invade the silence. He is casually dressed in jeans, striped polo shirt and Gucci loafers.

Big dogs bark O/S. He starts and a book on his knee slides to the floor. He wakes.

DIKELEDI (KELE) opens the door; light shines in from the lit passage. Her face is hidden by the enormous bunch of cherry blossom she is carrying and she's wearing yellow kitchen gloves.

LEKO peeks round the chair and changes his yawn to a ghostly sound, waving his arms about above the chairback.

LEKO: Woo! Woo! 'Ek is jou pappie se spook!' *[i.e.: 'I am your daddy's ghost']* or: I am the Spirit of Afrika!

KELE stops stock-still squealing with fright, the blossoms trembling. LEKO laughing, goes to switch on the light by the door.

LEKO: Sorry, Kele, it's only me…sorry.

KELE: Hé la! You scared me, Masopha man! U nkentse letswalo!

A stream of invective in Sotho.

KELE: What're you doing in here anyway? Why're you up so early? It's only half-four.

LEKO: I'm not 'up' – I slept here all bloody night. Me 'n' Leo were all set to go and roll out the red carpet for Lulu, but then we heard all domestic flights were suspended – Jo'burg is snow-bound, can you believe? Then suddenly there's a phone call saying they're fed up with waiting and they'll drive through the night. Typical Lulu. Hell, my neck is killing me.

KELE: Mampara! (*Dogs again.*) Listen, I swear that's them!

She opens one half of the shutters to look out of the window. A frosty morning light.

LEKO: Not yet. By the time they sorted her luggage, and hired the car, and argued the route… y'know the sort of thing. She's been overseas a whole five years; I'm wondering what she's like now. When I was a kid, fifteen or so, my father – dead and gone now – came here looking for work. He'd been drinking as usual, and he'd hit me and made my nose bleed. Shu! Lulu – *'Miss'* Lulu I called her then for heaven's sake! –

KELE meanwhile is arranging the blossoms in a big vase, dusting absent-mindedly and so on.

LEKO: … gave my father a job straight off. She took me into the kitchen and cleaned up the blood at the sink. 'What's your name?' she says. 'Alexander The Great, hey? Too grand – I shall call you Leko.' So Leko it's been. 'Don't cry, moshomane,' she says, 'the world will be yours one day.' She wasn't wrong – here I am now with a BiMa 7 and Guccis.

KELE: Wa-ikgantsha! ['Show-off!']

LEKO: Man, I *like* making money – I've got a knack for it. But I wonder sometimes if it's changed me? No, one thing's for sure I haven't forgotten my roots – oh no. (*Picks up the book from the floor.*) She'd say: 'Read this, Leko, it's *the* English play of all time'. 'Something rotten in the State…' hey? Sounds familiar. Ichu! – my neck. I should've moved to the sofa.

The dogs bark again.

KELE: The dogs were whining all night, like they know Miss Lulu is coming.

She sits suddenly on the sofa, peeling off her gloves.

LEKO: You OK, Dikeledi?

KELE: Heh, Masopha, look at my hands – all trembling. I think I'm going to faint.

LEKO: Now, Kele, don't you go all 'white' on me. And look at your painted nails, child, look at your shoes. Don't get any funny ideas…

KELE: Hé la, look who's talking – Mr Gucci shoes!

Enter KHOKOLOHO carrying a huge bunch of white hydrangeas. He walks awkwardly, the sole flapping on one of his trainers.

KHOKO: Isiah sent these in from the greenhouse, for the dining-room. The big copper vase, he says, that the madam specially likes.

LEKO: Any chance of a coffee, Kele? (*Teasing.*) Black and strong like me.

KELE: (*Returning the tease with a little mock curtsy.*) Eya, ntate!

Exit DIKELEDI with the hydrangeas. KHOKOLOHO watches her go.

KHOKO: Thick frost out there, and the cherry trees full of flowers. I don't think much of our wonderful climate when it does this – it muddles up my trees. (*He warms his hands and his feet.*) See this? (*Shows his flapping takkie.*) It's all vrot. I want some really strong boots. Maybe you've got some old ones, Masopha? Real leather like these, nê? (*He slips off one of LEKO's Guccis and smells the leather.*) Cho cho cho…

LEKO: You and your big feet. Loop, Khokoloho! (*Grabs his shoe.*)

KHOKO: So, OK OK – no harm to ask. I'm just out of luck, like always. (*He sits gloomily in a baby chair and addresses the teddy bear.*) But no complaints, I'm used to it. I just laugh, listen to this: hê, hê, hê…

LEKO: Khokoloho, you're crazy.

Enter KELE with a mug of coffee. When KHOKOLOHO tries to rise the little chair sticks to his butt.

KHOKO: Ichu! See what? – event the chair bites me. Cho cho…

She chases him out. Exit KHOKOLOHO

KELE: 'Disaster City' that one, that's what they call him in the township. 'Parathlathlé!' they call after him. Forever falling over and dropping things. He wants me for his wife, Masopha. It's a joke, I don't know what to do.

LEKO: Uh huh… (*Blowing on his coffee.*)

KELE: He's a quiet man, but once he gets going – no stopping him. Shame, he's such a clumsy ouk, and I think I even quite like him. But Mrs Disaster? Shu! – I don't think so.

O/S: The arrival of two cars, hooting cheerfully. The big dogs bark furiously.

LEKO: They've come!

KELE: I've got goose pimples. Look here!

LEKO: Cool it, Kele, calm down. Will she know me straight off, I wonder?

LEKO pulls on his jacket and Exits. O/S Voices, hubbub. KELE, babbling 'Miss Lulu, Miss Lulu!' with excitement, rushes about in a panic picking up the mug, her gloves, the duster, the book, taking off her apron, her doek, etc. Then Exits. Enter PUTSWA who crosses steadily to Anna's room with a vanity case, muttering quietly to himself. MARIA and ANNA burst in and run across to her room.

ANNA: (*Over her shoulder as she runs.*) Ma, Ma, remember this room?

Enter LULU and LEO (a dressing-gown over clothes.) followed by LEKO. Also KARLOTTA holding her little dog Boytjie, (or not), and PICKETT (carefully carrying a cake tin); and KELE with various duty-free bags.

LEO: Remember this room, Luly?

LULU: The nursery!

ANNA and MARIA come back from ANNA's room. LEKO helps LULU off with her coat.

LULU: How could I forget? My best room in the whole world! I slept just here when I was little. And my Marietjie just the same as ever – still in her Sunday best, I see. Did you miss your mommie, skattie?

MARIA: I've lit the fire in your rooms, Ma, they're nicely warmed up.

LULU: Oh no, it's never little Kele is it? (*KELE shyly approaches.*) Just look at you, all grown up and so pretty! (*She kisses her.*) Come here, girls.

LULU riffles through her duty-free bags and gives them presents. (KELE a coral necklace, MARIA, a big glossy book on the cathedrals of France). Meanwhile LEO addresses PICKETT.

LEO: The inland flights were grounded, y'know, by those idiots at Jo'burg. And for why? 'Ice on the wings' they said, and not a blowtorch in sight! Back to the Third World, hey Luly-pops? With a bump!

LEO grabs the scarf from her neck and they both run off like kids. MARIA and LEKO follow in their wake.

KARLOTTA: (*To PIK.*) My little dog likes monkey-nuts, jy weet? He can shell them with his teeth. Jus' like his mommie.

PIK: Well I never.

Exit KARLOTTA whistling for her dog.

KELE: Can you do this up for me?

ANNA does up the clasp of the necklace.

ANNA: Pretty.

PUTSWA returns from ANNA's room.

PUTSWA: My mosadinyana is home again, home again. I waited and waited for her, so now it's OK if I die.

PIK: I know the feeling old boy.

PUTSWA, not having heard properly, smiles and goes. PICKETT wanders out with his cake tin.

KELE: Anna, hey! I thought you'd never get here.

ANNA: On the move for two days and two nights, and not a wink. Hell, this is arctic! (*She decides to keep her coat on.*)

KELE: Not as cold as when you left last July – they had to close the mountain road the snow was so bad. Anna, I've got to tell you a big secret.

ANNA: (*Yawning.*) Now what?

KELE: Khokoloho had the cheek to speak to my father; he wants me for his wife. It's just so embarrassing.

ANNA: So what's new, Kele?

KELE: So what do I do? He loves me, he just loves me so much…

ANNA lights up and wanders into her room.

ANNA: (*from O/S.*) My own room, my own windows, my very own view, like I'd never left. (*She wanders back in.*) I can't wait to go outside. Wish I could sleep on planes.

KELE is riffling through the plastic bags and finds a T-shirt with 'I love Paris', which she puts on.

KELE: Pitso Thekiso showed up two days ago. Just like that – out of the blue.

ANNA: Never! Professor Pitso! I've not seen him since the day Gerrie died.

KELE: He said to be woken up when you got here, but Maria did her thing with the finger: 'Don't you wake him, my girl!' she says…

Enter MARIA.

MARIA: Dikeledi, Miss Lulu wants her Rooibos, now-now. Off you go.

KELE: Now-now, Miss Maria.

Exit KELE.

MARIA: Am I pleased you're back! My darling sister's home again – and smoking too much. Oos wes tuis bes, nê my skat?

ANNA: It's been pretty hellish, I can tell you. I wish you'd come with me instead of Lottie.

MARIA: How was I to leave Uncle all alone here? He's no good at alone, and worse with the staff.

ANNA: She kept showing off with her stupid conjuring tricks.

MARIA: There's no way Ma would let you travel on your own, Antjie.

ANNA: I know, I'm old enough to vote but I can't catch a plane on my own. Pathetic.

MARIA: And Ma…?

ANNA: Ma? – ja. Filthy weather when we arrive, plus she's taken a flat on the fifth floor and the lift is bust. I thought at least she'd be happy to see me, but the place is heaving – poetic types with long hair, and smart spiky ladies. French is so fast, I was lost. I suddenly felt sorry for Ma, so *so* sorry for her, and I took her in my arms and wouldn't let her go. When they all left Ma kept hugging me and crying as if her heart would break.

MARIA: Ah, shame… don't say more.

MARIA gets up, agitated.

ANNA: Even though she'd sold the villa at Menton, she still had nothing over – mentioned daylight robbery. She's hopeless – she insists on the most expensive restaurants and then tips everyone in sight, way over the odds. And Nyatso's become a total pain – he expects three-course meals three times a day. He and Lottie both. God, can she eat – she hoovers it up!

MARIA: They've got a nasty surprise coming.

ANNA: Tell me, how's things then? Is the interest paid off?

MARIA: You joke.

ANNA: Of course – silly me.

MARIA: Worse still; this coming February the bank's going to repossess and then sell the whole estate.

ANNA: No! Oh God!

MARIA: At auction!

ANNA: Oh God – this place. What'll we do?

LEKO sticks his head through the door and suddenly trumpets like an elephant, waving his arm like a trunk. Then goes.

MARIA: Ooh, he makes me so mad sometimes!

ANNA: But he fancies you, I swear. Pretend it's Leap Year and propose to him – go on, I dare you.

MARIA: He keeps popping in to see us on his travels, but he just looks at me like I'm not really there. Maybe he's shy, maybe he likes his bachelor life, maybe my colour…

ANNA: No! I think he's deep down just an old tribalist at heart, for all it's the new South Africa and Rainbow Nation and silly elephants and stuff.

MARIA: Well, to hell with him! Ma didn't give a hoot about gossip when they adopted me. Though I guess she loved Pa so much she'd do just anything for his sake.

ANNA hugs MARIA.

ANNA: No, Marietjie, no. She loved you for *you.*

MARIA: And when you were born, I got a baby sister en daar is ons. Same father different skin. So what?

ANNA: (*Gently.*) So what?

MARIA: I miss Pa often… Did you miss me in Paris? Your brooch looks a little bee.

ANNA: We found it in a flea market.

MARIA looks at the pictures in her new book, concentrating.

MARIA: The colour thing doesn't just go away like overnight, you know. Yiss, look at that! Looks just like me.

ANNA: Oh, yeah, the spit. You silly. Those gargoyles are actually drains, did you know?

MARIA: Me, I don't give a damn who I marry so long as there's love.

ANNA: And there's Chartres – Lottie and I took a bus. (*As she goes to her room.*) We also took the Eurostar to London – there and back in a day. So cool.

Enter KELE with a tray and sets it out on the coffee table.

MARIA: I keep dreaming you'll find some to-die for zillionaire and save us all…

ANNA: (*From O/S.*) No *thank* you!

MARIA: ...and then we could travel the world and walk through great cities – Paris, Rome – walk and walk – and then come home and have lots and lots of babies.

ANNA: (*From O/S.*) The birds are going nuts in the orchard. What's the time?

MARIA: Five-ish. I'll turn down your bed.

Exit MARIA into ANNA's room. Enter NYATSO carrying ANNA's suitcase.

NYATSO: OK to go through here?

KELE: Heh, Nyatso – I didn't know who you were for a sec. You've changed a lot.

NYATSO: (*Dumps down the suitcase.*) And who exactly are you?

KELE: I'm the daughter of Thabo Moletsane – Dikeledi. When you left I was so high. You won't remember me.

NYATSO: What a lekker little cherry, *chérie.*

He laughs at his pun and pinches her on the butt; KELE screams and drops a saucer. Enter MARIA. Exit NYATSO quickly.

MARIA: Yes? So what's going on?

KELE: Oh, Miss Maria, I dropped a saucer.

Enter ANNA.

MARIA: OK, OK, I won't bite your head off.

Exit DIKELEDI.

ANNA: Shouldn't we tell Ma that Pitso's turned up?

MARIA: Not yet, not yet.

ANNA: Remember how we used to take Pa his breakfast coffee and there they both were, closeted in the study, plotting away? Then he was gone. Wish I knew what they'd been up to.

MARIA: Maybe just as well you didn't.

ANNA: Pa died six years ago and, just four weeks later, Gerrit. Only seven years old and drowned, gone for ever. That lovely little brother of ours, just gone. For ever. Ma couldn't take it, but now I can see why she did that, leaving us for so long, and I find I can absolutely forgive it. You?

MARIA, silent, takes the suitcase into ANNA's room, then returns.

ANNA: The day Gerrie died, Pitso was around on one of his flying visits, remember? He found him in the dam. How Gerrie worshipped Pitso, followed him around like a puppy, jabbering away in Sotho. Marietjie, it will all come back when she sees him – really, we ought to tell her.

Enter PUTSWA.

PUTSWA: Mosadinyana wants her Rooibos, is it ready? Heh, wena! (*Calling DIKELEDI, who Enters.*) Where's the water jug, mosetsane? Ngoan'o ke sethoto…

KELE: Ohmygod! (*Goes out quickly.*)

PIK, clutching his cake tin, wanders in.

MARIA: What's so funny, Putswa?

PUTSWA: Paris, hey? The master had many many friends in that place – all exiles. Now they can come home, it's safe.

Enter LULU, LEO, LEKO.

LULU: How's it done? The yellow into the corner, then I double into the middle?

LEO: Nope, screw-shot into the corner. God! We used to sleep in this room, Luly, you and I, and now all of a sudden – pham! – I'm getting on for sixty. Where's it all gone?

LEKO: Yes, time waits for no man…

LEO: What was that?

LEKO: (*Murmuring.*) Yes-no, I just said 'time'…

LEO: There's a smell of – what? – bloody poncey aftershave, is it?

ANNA: Must kip. 'Night all, 'morning I mean. (*Kisses LULU.*)

LULU: Happy to be back, aren't you my angel? Me too. I have to pinch myself.

LEO: Sleep tight, mind the bugs don't bite. (*Kisses ANNA.*) Just look at her, Luly, she's the spit of you at her age.

Exit ANNA, waving goodnight to LEKO and 'Uncle' PIK. Enter KELE with a silver water jug, puts it on the tray, goes.

LULU: Annie's worn out, little thing.

PIK: Well, it's quite a ways.

MARIA: Well, gents, going-home time, I'd say.

LULU: You never change, Maria, do you my little gauleiter? I'll just have my tea and then bed. (*PUTSWA fusses with cushions.*) Bless you, old friend. (*Sipping the Rooibos.*) Oh but that's good! D'you know you can get this overseas now? Expats can't live without it, apparently. (*She spies the* Hamlet *on the coffee table.*) Well, well, who's the bookworm?

LEKO sidles over and relieves her of it. Enter KHOKOLOHO who whispers in MARIA's ear.

MARIA: Ma, I'll check if all your bags're upstairs.

Exit MARIA and KHOKOLOHO.

LULU: Is this actually me? In this very room? (*Laughs.*) What if it's all a dream? God knows, I love my country, love it! When I peered out of the plane at Africa, dappled like a huge old leopard, the tears kept coming, so not a thing could I see. Plus I had to sing all night to keep Anna awake at the wheel – I exhausted my repertoire. What a wreck! Putswa, old thing, I'm so happy you're still with us.

PUTSWA: Letsatsi pela maubane. *[i.e.: the day before yesterday]*

LEO: With us but not with us – deaf as a bloody post.

LEKO: I must be on my way soon. Shame, I'd like to stick around and talk to you about – oh, this and that. You're looking fine, great in fact.

PIK: Better than ever – very 'chick' – quite sets the pulses racing. (*Helping himself to a cup of Rooibos.*) Can't stand this stuff – too healthy by half.

He joins LEO, who is watching CNN News on the TV, sound low.

LEKO: (*Teasing.*) That brother of yours, old Guyver there, still can't get the hang of a black man with brains. Makes him uneasy.

LULU: He's a terrible old stick-in-the-mud, Leko. What's one to do?

LEKO: Such talks we had in this room during the dark days – politics, politics, every breath was politics. Now it's all money – gravy-trains and money…

PIK: And crime…

LEKO: Hell! I miss him, your old man.

Looking at the portrait of Johan.

LULU: Ah, Leko – don't.

LEKO: I know, I know, sorry. Funny thing, life – my father used to wait at your table and now the tables have turned…

LULU: … and none too soon.

LEKO: If I can be of any use to you…? I owe you, you and Johan.

LULU: Nothing, dearest Leko, you owe nothing. Imagine the joy it gave us to give you a leg-up. If that Big Baby over there had been clever enough he could also have done an MBA. Not so, Leo? (*LEO remains oblivious at the TV.*) Ouf! I can't keep still. Bookcases! Bookcases!

She runs to kiss one bookcase and across to the other, just as KHOKOLOHO comes in, carrying a case to ANNA's room. They collide. She's recovered in a trice.

LULU: Table! Desk! Teddy! Hello to you all!

KHOKOLOHO Exits to ANNA's room with the case.

LEO: Old Gogo died – did I say?

LULU: Darling nanny. Yes, you wrote to tell me, goofy.

LEO: Newberry of Prynnsberg died too, poor fellow. And Gert Pienaar – remember the bloke with the glass eye? – joined the police force. Good riddance. (*To PIK.*) I'm training up Khokoloho, y'know, he's got it up here. He'll manage the place for us one day.

Re-enter KHOKOLOHO, without the case, who stops when he hears his name, but LEO waves him off. Exit KHOKOLOHO.

PIK: Bit of affirmative action, what?

LEO: Yes, actually. He's damned thorough.

PIK: The slow slide into chaos, old chap. (*He finally gets to present his cake tin.*) Daughter Daphne sends her best.

LULU: Ah, melktert! No one makes it like she does. How lovely!

LULU and LEO tuck in with relish.

LEKO: I see I'll have to grab the bull by the horns.

LULU: You look good on it, Pik. Leko, have some?

LEKO: Look, people, I know Lulu says 'no', but I owe you, I do. The bank's all set to repossess the entire estate, orchard and all, and – no don't stop me – the sale's to take place at the end of the summer. You know that, don't you?

LULU: Leo, is this true?

LEKO: But there is a way out. The MBA has been thinking and he's come up with a Master Plan! Pay attention, folks: if the cherry orchard and the land lying alongside the Caledon River were cut into plots of, say, a hundred square metres, and a luxury cottage built on each – all mod cons – they could be leased out for holidays, or time-shares, or what. You could attract an income in excess of a million per annum. Probably more.

LEO: Sorry, what rubbish – bloody rubbish!

LULU: I'm not with you.

LEKO: But the cherry orchard will have to go, you understand, cut down to make room. But for a million…

LULU: 'Scuse me? 'Go'? 'Have to *go*'? What can you be thinking of, Alex my friend? Leo is right; it's out of the question.

LEO: There's only one remarkable thing in this entire godforsaken province and that's our cherry orchard!

LEKO: There's only one remarkable thing about your cherry orchard: its size. Shu – you two are such little ostriches! A reminder perhaps? Now where are his memoirs? (*He finds a book on a shelf.*) A self-made man – I've read this dozens of times. Your great-grandfather, twenty-three years old, sailed into Durban in 1864, to seek his fortune. 'I had nothing,' he says here. 'I had nothing but my hands and my brain.' Off he went to Kimberley when they discovered the diamonds, slept in a shack, and scrabbled in the earth for seven whole years. By 'seventy-nine he'd become so rich he could buy more shares in the new De Beers than Cecil John Rhodes himself.

LEO eats more tart.

LEKO: And who helped him to get so rich? One guess. Eya, where would you be without us, I wonder? So then what did he do? Why, buy land of course, like they all did. Lots and lots of it – all along this lovely river and back to the krans behind. Three thousand hectares of prime grazing land was his for a song. Land once belonging to the Basotho people – my people, our land. So then he found a wife, he built this house and he planted his glorious orchard. And four generations of dear little Guyvers thought life would be like that for ever. But things have changed, wouldn't you say? And a lousy crop every second year is not what you'd call a living. You can't eat blossoms, dammit!

45

LEO steams up to the shelves and brandishes another book.

LEO: That orchard, I'll have you know, has a double spread in *Scenes from the Orange Republic.*

LEKO: Think about it. Next February great-grandpa starts revolving in his grave – unless you listen to me.

PUTSWA: Long time ago – forty, fifty years – they dried them, soaked them, marinaded them, made jam…

LEO: Shush, Putswa.

PUTSWA: …and in a good year we sent over big ox-wagons full of cherries for the Festival in Ficksburg. We made profits then, our cherries were juicy like plums, crispy like apples. Hé la, in those days we had our methods for jams, very special methods, with builder's lime…

LULU: No, that's for preserved figs, I think. (*Raising her voice.*) Who knows these 'methods' now, Putswa?

PUTSWA: Gogo knows it… I forget.

LULU: All forgotten, how sad.

LEKO: That orchard is barren! This house is too big!

An uncomfortable silence.

PIK: Did you eat well in Paris? Did you try frogs?

LULU: Certainly not! Squid.

PIK: Clever damn things those; saw one showing off once. They put a jam jar in his tank; with one foot he holds it, with another he unscrews the top, with a thirds he hoiks out his food and there's another left over to wave at us. I tell you we clapped like hell. The aquarium raked it in!

LEO: Octopus you mean, old boy, not squid.

LEKO: Look here, there'll be a big demand for new holiday markets – not everyone wants the seaside. Fear not, we'll do nothing vulgar – not another Vaal Dam.

LEO: Perish the thought!

LEKO: Just so. River frontage, luxurious cottages, plots big enough to make them feel special. I tell you, he'll sit on his stoep of an evening, a cool Castle in his hand, watching the sun go down, and he'll want to cultivate his little plot – maybe plant a tree for the children and hey presto! – a new cherry orchard!

LEO: Did you hear that, Luly?

LULU: Did I, indeed.

Enter MARIA with fresh flowers and envelopes, NYATSO following.

MARIA: I forgot, Ma, two faxes for you, came yesterday.

LULU: From Paris. (*To LEO.*) I'm done with Paris.

She doesn't read them. MARIA puts the flowers in a vase.

LEO: Luly, I found a date burned into the wood here. Bet you don't know how old these bookshelves are? One hundred years, how's about that, then? We should toast their centenary – they'd be chuffed don't you think? Putswa, some drinks.

Exit PUTSWA followed by NYATSO.

PIK: Good thinking, old boy.

During this speech, PIK drops off to sleep and snores gently; LULU and MARIA get the giggles.

LEO: And the white ants haven't got them yet! Honoured bookshelves, revered bookshelves – you've stood here for generations offering up to curious minds your myriad treasures. Your constant plea for open minds silently beckons us. Your unflagging call for fruitful labours, for a social conscience, for faith in a brighter future, have at last been answered. We salute the new democracy. How does it go? Amandhla! (*He raises his fist awkwardly in the freedom salute.*)

LEKO: (*Raising his in reply.*) Ngawethu! In truth, those bookcases helped me to change my life. Bayete, bookcase!

LEKO drops to one knee, arms stretched forward Zulu-fashion, gently aping a royal salutation.

LULU: Pull the other one, Leo, darling. Since when did you give a fig about democracy?

Enter NYATSO with a tray; PUTSWA following. KARLOTTA has come in to listen and sits smoking on the window seat.

LEO: Pham! Screw-shot into the pocket. A toast!

LEKO: Not me, I should be on my way.

NYATSO: Your pills, *chére madame.* (*Offering the tray to LULU.*)

PIK: You musn't take drugs, dearest Lulu. The body has a tendency to get better, they say. Let's have a gander. Beta-blockers, hey? Away with you! (*He blows on the pills and swallows them.*) There!

LULU: You're off your head! You'll get sick!

MARIA: (*Thumping his back.*) Uncle Pik, you're mad!

PIK: Not a bit of it; I need calming down – Lulu does that to a chap.

LEKO: Greedy guy.

PUTSWA: U ja haholo – nako tsole *[i.e.: He always eats a lot].*

LULU: What now, Putswa?

MARIA: He's been muttering for years now. We ignore it.

NYATSO: Ngunu is ready for his ancestors.

KARLOTTA helps herself to the melktert.

LEKO: Ah, die liewe Karlotta, welcome back! Would you call this a French kiss? (*Tries to kiss her hand.*)

KARLOTTA: Ag nee, skande, M'sieu Aleksander! One thing leads to another, jy weet. Oppas!

LEKO: Never, ma'm'selle! Karlotta! Will you show us a trick?

KARLOTTA: Abracadabra – abracadabra – abracadabra…
(*She balances the cake tin on her fingertips, sashays to the door.*)
abracadabra – I've gone to bed!

Exit KARLOTTA. Applause.

LEKO: I must vanish too – see you in three weeks or so. (*Kisses
LULU's hand.*) *You'll* allow me, won't you? (*Teasing LEO.*)
Stay well, my democratic friend. (*Wry, to PIK.*) Comrade!
(*To PUTSWA.*) Sala hantle, ngunu. (*Back to LULU.*) When you
make up your minds about the y'know – and I strongly
suggest you do soonest – I'd be happy to advance you
whatever you require. Planning takes time. Absolutely no
strings.

MARIA: Well, *go* if you're going, for heaven's sake!

LEKO: Eya, – I'm off. Shu! Musn't forget the office.

*He swerves back to pick up his briefcase, another swerve to the desk
to pick up Hamlet, and Exit LEKO. A silence.*

LEO: Money, money, money – he bores for Africa!

LULU: Leo, Leo, Leo…

LEO: But what does he think he's doing, interfering like this?

LULU: Now just stop it. He wants to help.

LEO: Oops! Pardon – Maria's got her eye on him.

MARIA: Who says? Uncle, you are terrible.

LULU: Have you now? Wonderful! He's a good man.

PIK: Got his ear to the ground, that one. But he's unusual for
a – y'know what I mean…

MARIA turns away sharply. A raised eyebrow from LULU.

PIK: Daphne holds a candle for him too. She says – she says –
well, lots of things. Neewat, horses for courses… (*He drops
off for a second in his chair.*)

LULU: (*Quietly to MARIA.*) Darling – they're too old to adjust.

49

MARIA: (*Furious.*) But how can he even think like that?

LULU: He does his best. Lord, what a world!

PIK: (*Wakes.*) Oh damn! Tomorrow the interest on my bond must be paid. You couldn't, dear lady, loan me…?

MARIA: Don't even think about it, Ma. No!

She goes into ANNA's room.

LULU: Pik, old chou, I don't have a sou.

PIK: Just asked. I'm an optimist mostly. Something'll crop up; maybe Daphne will win the lottery.

LULU: I'm drowning in Rooibos, enough's enough. Bed.

PUTSWA: What shall I do with you, Mr Leo, heh? You should be dressed properly for the madam.

Enter MARIA; opens the other shutter. Bright morning sunlight streams in.

MARIA: Antjie's dead to the world. Good, it's warming up, the sun's higher. Come look, Ma, at our trees and my God, the air! Sharp and clear. (*She has opened the window.*) Just listen to those turtle-doves.

LULU joins MARIA at the window.

LEO: The orchard's all white, white, white – glorious. Remember the long avenue, Luly, shining on a moonlit night 'like a silver sword', we used to say. Remember? You've not forgotten?

LULU: Childhood. Yes, so vivid, images burned into the mind. Each morning my eyes would spring open to – this ocean of white. It's all just as I remember. You're a ravishing orchard, oh yes, you are! All virginal white like a blushing bride – shady in summer, naked in winter – and now, bursting with life all over again. I wish I were a tree, I wish I could drop my thoughts like winter leaves.

LEO: And it's that orchard that someone not a million miles away wants us to chop down.

LULU: Oh, look – Mama all in white walking in the orchard. Look!

LEO: What? Where?

LULU: To the left, by the path to the tennis courts – the little white tree bending over – looks just like a woman stooping to kiss a little child.

MARIA: Oh Ma, don't – it's spooky.

LULU: No, of course, darling, no one there. Just me dreaming.

PITSO THEKISO looks through the window from the outside and taps gently on the glass.

LULU: Who's that?

PITSO: Ma Rademeyer – hi! Good to see you. I was told not to come over, but, like, I can't wait. Good to see you.

MARIA: It's Pitso, Ma, Piet Thekiso

LULU sits, shocked.

PITSO: I'm still 'Piet' to you, I guess, but I use my African name now. You don't remember? Oh, wow, I must look weird or something. Meneer Rademeyer helped me with my law degree, and I taught Gerrie Sotho and stuff.

LULU: Pietie? My God! (*Cries.*)

Exit MARIA.

LEO: Hey, hey, Luly, gently does it, old girl.

MARIA's voice O/S as she lets him in: 'What did I tell you, Pitso? I said tomorrow – tomorrow!

Enter PITSO followed by MARIA.

LULU: My Gerrie… my little boy… my love… my son. Drowned, dead – why? Why? (*She strikes out wildly at PITSO, just as suddenly stops.*) Oh Piet, I'm so sorry, so sorry. No one's fault, no one's. Anna's fast asleep and here I am shouting away – making a terrible noise. But Piet…

PITSO: Pitso.

LULU: Pitso, sorry – you've grown all serious somehow. Last time I saw you – fire in the belly and lots of hair. Now you're wearing specs and a little touch of grey right here. Surely you're still not a student?

PITSO: I'm due to finish my law degree, soon as my grant comes through. So I'm doing some writing to fill in.

LULU: Better than being on the run.

PITSO: I guess so. Got a deadline to meet, must be off tonight.

LULU: That's my Pitso – always off into the night. Enough for one day, a nap I think. Oh dear, we're none of us spring chickens any more, are we, brother mine?

PIK: Ouch! Eina! The old hip's acting up. I'll stay over, if that's OK? And after your beauty sleep, my beauty, perhaps you could see your way to…

LEO: His bloody bond!

PIK: I'll pay it back in a jiffy – my word is my bond, ho-ho.

LULU: Oh, let's live dangerously! How's about it, Leo?

LEO: Sure thing, how much would he like? Name your figure, Pik, old son. Anything goes.

LULU: Be a devil – go on, Scroogie.

LEO: Nothing doing.

Exit LULU, followed by PITSO, PIK and PUTSWA.

LEO: That sister of mine just chucks the bread about, like feeding ducks! (*To NYATSO.*) There's a whiff of Parisian henhouse round here, m'boy. *Poulet de luxe,* what?

NYATSO: (*Grins.*) It's good to see you're the same as ever, Mr Leo.

LEO: Cheeky bugger.

MARIA: Your mother's been waiting in the back for hours, Nyatso. She's walked all the way from Thaba Nchu to see you.

NYATSO: Trust her.

MARIA: You are shameless – that's no way to behave.

NYATSO: Who needs it?

Exit NYATSO with his tray.

MARIA: Always the same old story; if I didn't stop her she'd just give everything away.

LEO: She already bloody has – to that swine in Paris. Give, give, give – Lucy's chronic condition. One of us, no name no pack-drill, had better go and be very *very* nice to Great-Aunt Newlands. She is positively rolling and hopefully near death.

MARIA: Uncle, how could you?

LEO: Don't blubber, there's a good girl. She's never forgiven Luly for falling for a penniless Dutchman instead of some chinless aristo – an advocate and, worse still, a Commie, and there's nothing more liberal *[alt: 'verlig']* than a lapsed Afrikaner. Big mistake, Auntie cut the phone wires. But since Rademeyer died…

MARIA: Just a month before Gerrie – oh God, no wonder she ran…

LEO: Your pa was a fine fellow – be proud. I think she *needs* to be in love. Paris, y'know, and that succubus who bleeds her dry. Luly, no getting round it, is a feckless little number…

Enter ANNA in pyjamas.

MARIA: (*Whispering.*) Watch it.

LEO: Hey? (*Pause.*) Strange thing – got a speck in my right eye. I was at the Court of Appeal last Thursday and…

MARIA: Why've you woken up, Antjie?

53

ANNA shrugs, looking straight at LEO.

LEO: My little Annie, sweet Annie – you're not just my niece, you're my angel, my treasure, my sweetheart…

ANNA: OK, OK, I love you too, Uncle. But frankly, my mother is not your business.

LEO: No, look here, Annie – it's because your mother's damned affair has finally broken the camel's back.

ANNA: Just leave her alone, Uncle! You've got foot-in-mouth disease, is what.

LEO: I know, I know, stupid speeches to bookcases… I'm silent, I promise. Just one thing, though…

BOTH: *Uncle!*

LEO: No, look here girls. I was at a bit of a 'do' at the Appellate Courts in Bloem last Thursday and got chatting to various legal eagles, and just maybe we can arrange something. The estate's been entailed for a hundred years, but now with me, for the first time it's out of constraint. I could maybe remortgage in my lifetime?

ANNA: Oh, yeah, re-*re*mortgage – you'd be dead lucky.

MARIA: Oh God.

LEO: (*To MARIA.*) You're blubbing again. (*To ANNA.*) I've got to calm the bank down somehow. Annie, I want you to pay your respects to Great-Aunt Newlands – you're in her good books. She's family, she should bloody help, dammit!

ANNA: I'm not going to toady.

LEO: You're her golden girl, Annie. Persuade her to buy it for you, put it in trust for you, whatever. (*Glancing at MARIA.*) For you both, I mean. Hey, no blubbering!

MARIA: It's just I can't bear it might be sold to not family. I dream of us bringing our children here, like us, for ever.

LEO: Cross my heart, the estate will be safe. So we'll mount the attack on both fronts – the horns of the ox, hey? I smell victory. (*Eats a sweet.*) Wragtig! Call me an old gasbag if I let it go to auction. Here's my hand on it – c'mon girls, give me five.

MARIA ignores his hand. ANNA gives it a desultory whack.

ANNA: (*Wry.*) Oh, I'll be able to sleep like a baby now.

MARIA: But why won't you listen to Leko's ideas?

LEO: Don't mention Leko's damned ideas! He's got nothing to do with this estate. Anyway he's…

Enter PUTSWA.

PUTSWA: Heh, Master Leo, when are you going to dress? Shesha!

LEO: I'll see to myself, Putswa. It's OK, I c'n manage, old boy. Well, children, more tomorrow. Lekker slaap, my chook.

He kisses ANNA, then turns at the door.

LEO: Yes, a child of the fifties, that's me. Not a decade held in much esteem 'cept for Elvis, but I can tell you I've done my fair share of protest.

Hoots of derision.

LEO: No, believe me, girls, letting Rademeyer live here, carrying on with his bloody Commie activities, putting us all in danger, is nothing to sniff at. Which is why the staff all trust me. Yup, you have to know how to deal with your Affs…

ANNA: Uncle Leo, you can't speak like that! Its bloody insulting, is what!

MARIA: And Putswa here – it's just awful!

She weeps with sheer rage. PUTSWA hasn't heard.

PUTSWA: Mr Leo – shesha!

LEO: Coming, coming. Pot the white, cushion into the middle.

Exit LEO and PUTSWA. ANNA yawns.

ANNA: So I must go off to Capetown and suck up to the great-aunt, must I? Eina!

MARIA: Hey no, don't! (*ANNA pulls MARIA on to her lap.*) Oh, by the way, something not very nice went on while you were away. Remember the oldies staying on in the stable block? Matla, Sanna, Tshepo and of course darling old Selena?

ANNA: (*Sleepy.*) Darling old Selena...

MARIA: Well, odds and sods from the squatter camp used to sleep over every now and then, but I just let it ride. So then I hear on the grapevine that I'd ordered they should be given nothing, not even puthu, because I was so, like, mean, y'know? And it turned out Tshepo was fanning the flames. Okidokey, I said to myself, you gonna get it, my boy, right in the neck. I send for him. He shows up – butter wouldn't melt. 'What game are you playing?' I ask him. 'You should be grateful for shelter,' I say. Hey, Antjie? Out like a light. Off we go then. (*She helps ANNA to her feet and starts walking her to her room.*) Nearly there, sweetheart, go easy, hanyane, hanyane...

PITSO peeks his head in the door.

PITSO: I think I left my cap...

MARIA: Shush. Come, skattie...

ANNA: I'm so tired, keep hearing engines 'night Ma sleep tight mind the bugs don't bite.

She catches sight of PITSO and raises a hand in greeting, but MARIA steers her out.

MARIA: Come, sweetheart, nearly there.

Exit ANNA and MARIA.

PITSO finds his baseball cap on a bookshelf; looks towards ANNA's closed door.

PITSO: *Solnyshko mayó, moy vesényi tsvetóchek...*

He runs out.

End of Act One.

Act Two

Early February, sunset time on the veld, close to the dam.

A wind-pump, its head turning slowly. A big sky behind. Two deckchairs DSR; SC a log with clothes and towels thrown over it. On a rug, a cold box and a tin bucket with bottles sticking out of it. US: a hill with a rusty plough; the path to the main house runs behind it.

KHOKOLOHO is perched on the plough playing his imbira (or a mouth organ). Next to him a tin of Coca-Cola, from which he occasionally swigs. [This is optional: Suddenly there is a gunshot and the Coke tin flies in the air. KHOKOLOHO yells with fright.]

Enter KARLOTTA, a shotgun in one hand and carrying a dead hasie by its ears. KHOKOLOHO swears at her. She whistles for her dog Boytjie; takes a bottle from the ice-bucket, sits on the log and drinks thirstily. KHOKOLOHO calms down and plays to himself again. KARLOTTA takes a small ID from her top pocket. She talks to herself; we feel she often does.

KARLOTTA: My ID tells me everything I know about myself. I'm just a number with a name attached. Whose name, girlie? Is it really mine or did the orphanage invent it? Did they invent when I was born as well, or just the day they found me? Sommer under a ou doring-boom? In a gutter? They never said. And who were my parents; were they married? I know nothing. One fine day Boswell-Wilkie's Circus comes to town and – big treat – all us kids is taken to see it. I cried at the animals, foeitog die arme diertjies. But hey! – there was this conjuror who was magic. Looked like the devil himself – long black moustachios. I wanted to be like him so bad. But what did they make me instead? A blerrie kindergarten teacher. Neewat, kids and dogs is OK. So then they took me on when old Rademeyer needed his briefs typing up; I asked no questions. So here I stay. But since Meneer dies who's there to talk with? Now Anna's busy with university and Maria's just a – just a big cry-baby. There's nobody. *(To the photo in her I.D.)* Can you hear me girlie?

KHOKOLOHO mockingly sings an Afrikaans love song, and after a bit she joins in with a quavering contralto:

KHOKO: *O my Sarie Marais is so ver van my hart*
Ek hoop om haar weer te sien
Daar onder in die meelies by die groen doring-boom
Daar woon my Sarie Marais.
O bring my terug na die ou Transvaal
Daar waar my Sarie woon…

KELE and NYATSO run on from the dam, he in trunks. The mood is broken.

KARLOTTA: (*To KHOKO.*) Ons sing net soos 'n jakals, awoo, awoo.

KHOKO: Some days I'm like a tree in a storm and pah! – the lightning strikes me. Why not another tree? I could be wrong, but then why, when I woke up this morning, do I see on my chest a huge great baboon-spider sitting there? Big like this! Just looking at me. Or when I drink some beer, why does a gogga always fly in for a swim? (*Pause.*) Karlotta, tell me, have you read all of the Bible?

No reply. KELE only has eyes for NYATSO as she sits on the rug, watching him while he pulls on his clothes. Upset by this, KHOKOLOHO changes tune to something harsher, slowly advancing on NYATSO as he sings. (The first and last line of the song means: 'Take your things and go'.)

KHOKO: *Vat jou goed en trek Ferreira, Jannie met die hoepel been*
Ein, zwei, drei, Ferreira
Ay yay yay, Ferreira
Ein, zwei, drei Ferreira
Vat jou goed en trek.

KHOKO: (*To NYATSO – a threat.*) Disasters can come at any time, don't you find?

KELE: 'Specially when they sing. More stories, Nyatso, go on, more, more. I wish I could go overseas too, lucky you.

NYATSO: Yeah, well, you guys live in the dark ages.

KHOKO: So. But they have had the time to work things out over there. Africa takes her own time.

NYATSO: Don't I know it. I choose to speak only English now – the world language. French when I'm in France, of course, but English here and everywhere.

KARLOTTA: Get him!

KHOKO: Well, I speak maybe four languages. I can read (*KELE hoots*)... I can! Standard Three was enough to teach me to...

KELE: It is not, Khokoloho, our schooling was kak.

KHOKO: ... but no books can tell me what I *really* want to know; like, do I go on like I am now, or must I go somewhere far, far away and find another life? So, I just play my tunes and I sing my songs.

He nearly sits on KARLOTTA's gun. They all scream. She grabs it.

KARLOTTA: I hear you, Khokoloho. You're a deep one, jy weet, and very smart. Not like him (*Indicating NYATSO.*) who jus' thinks he's clever. So, off I go. Always alone. And who I am, why I am, nobody knows.

Exit KARLOTTA, whistling for Boytjie.

KHOKO: Dikeledi, please, can you and me have a little talk?

KELE: Go on, then.

KHOKO: Can it be just the two of us?

KELE: OK, then. But first, can you get me my sweater? It's in my room – it'll be cold in a bit.

KHOKO: There you are – lightning! Pa-pham!

Exit KHOKOLOHO mournfully singing.

KELE: Am I too hard on him? He's a sweet guy but...

NYATSO: (*Lighting his cigar.*) Disaster City.

KELE: I've become such a worrier – too much time in the big house with whitey. Nothing is straight with them; they're always feeling guilty about who they are. Me, I *know* who I am, but also, I want – 'things'.

NYATSO: Little cherrie! (*A perfunctory kiss.*) Look, Kele, get smart; the guilt is because they're liberals. Play on it.

KELE: Nyatso, you know lots, don't you? You make me see things clearer.

NYATSO: For sure, I'm sorted out. Tell you what else I think – don't go and lose your head. Stay cool, like me. I don't go for loose women. (*KELE gives a small cry; hides her face in her hands.*) Mmm, cigars in the open air taste so good…

Sound of voices O/S.

NYATSO: Sh! Eya, it's them. Run! Or she'll find us together and get funny ideas. (*NYATSO pulls her to her feet.*) Run! That way, by the dam.

KELE: (*He puffs smoke at her.*) Your cigar *stinks*!

Exit DIKELEDI. NYATSO quickly knocks the head off his cigar, pockets it and opens a thermos of iced martini.

LEKO: (*V/O as they approach.*) It's dead simple; either you agree to leasing out your land, or you don't. Yes or no?

Enter LULU and LEKO, followed by LEO.

LULU: Who's been smoking cigars around here – little skellum.

LEO: One hour forty door to door – thank God no speed traps. We shot into town…

LULU: Shot is the operative…

LEO: … for a longish lunch; very congenial. (*Accepts a glass from NYATSO.*) Ah, good – a post-prandial. Yellow into the middle. Think I'll just scoot back for a quick game.

LULU: There's time, there's time…

LEKO: One word only. Make it 'yes'.

LULU: Yesterday my purse was full, today nary a tickey. Oh, where does it all go? My poor Maria has banned meat, so we get the frugal soups, while the poor staff are stuck with plain puthu. She's turning us all into vegans! And, oh dear, wasting my money on a senseless lunch… *wasting* it. How could I? Oops-a-daisy! (*She drops her purse; the coins scatter.*)

NYATSO: Allow me.

NYATSO starts picking up the coins.

LULU: *Merci,* Nyatso, *trop gentil.* Just look at that sun – the best time of the day. Bloemfontein is a cauldron, Leo, one should never travel for luncheon. And that ghastly lawyers' den you chose to eat in – vile muzak and the napkins reeked of stale Sunlight Soap.

LEO: Wise to keep in with the legal boys, I always think – never know when you'll need 'em.

LULU: And why eat so much, Leo? Why drink so much, why talk so much? All that maudlin nonsense about the Sixties and the 'Permissive Society'. It wasn't permissive in this benighted country, that's for sure. Those poor patient Portugoose waiters were yawning their heads off. Me too. No idea of time, have you? You're a real old African.

LEO: Apologies, sister mine.

LEKO: Modimo mphe pelo e telle! *[i.e.: God give me patience!]*

LEO: (*To NYATSO, searching for coins.*) What are you, a creepie-crawlie or what? Get out from under my feet!

NYATSO: (*Grinning.*) Another drink, Mr Leo?

LEO: Cheeky beggar! It's him or me…

LULU: *Tu peux t'en aller,* Nyatso – we can manage.

NYATSO: (*He hands the purse back to LULU.*) *Je m'en vais.*

He saunters off, lighting up his cigar butt on the way.

LEKO: Klippie Wessels has his eye on this estate, did you know?

LULU: And where did that come from?

LEKO: I keep my ear to the ground.

LULU: Little vessels and big ears…

LEO: Oh, honestly, Luly! No, Great-Aunt Newlands has agreed to cough up something. Antjie spent weeks buttering her up.

LEKO: And what d'you think she's prepared to part with? A hundred grand? Less? More? What?

LULU: Hardly – we'll be lucky to see fifty. More like ten, If I know her.

LEO: Where's your optimism, Luly? I've got high hopes.

LEKO: Sethoto! You're hopeless, you two. I tell you in the plainest language that your estate's going up in smoke, but you both refuse to take it in! Why? Why is this?

LULU: Naked terror, probably, Leko. Tell us, dear friend, what are we to do?

LEKO: But I keep telling you! My plan would give you, minimum, a million rand a year. You simply cannot afford to delay any longer!

LULU sighs; LEO gulps his drink.

LEKO: Look, if it's any comfort to you, you are not the only ones with a problem; those clever Evans's at Viljoenskroon are starting an adventure dome on their land, jungles and water-shutes and suchlike. They'll absolutely clean up, I tell you.

LULU: (*To LEO.*) All rather sordid, don't you find?

LEO: Couldn't be worse.

LEKO: I've had it, I wash my hands! (*To LEO.*) Wena, u mo mosadimoholo!

LEO: What was that?

LEKO: (*Collects his jacket, strides away, and shouts.*)
Mosadimoholo! You're an old woman!

LULU: (*Leaps up to fetch him back, puts her arm through his.*) No,
stay, I beg of you. I feel cheerier with you around. (*Pause.*)
I keep expecting something terribly dramatic – like the
house crashing down round our ears.

LEO: The red into the corner…

LEKO: It might – it just might!

LULU: I'm going to pay for my sins, I can feel it…

LEKO: Your only sin, my sister, is being stupid!

LEO: (*Eats a sweet.*) Oh well, chew up my fortune in chocolates.

LULU: Oh, such sins… My poor husband dies of drink and of
grief, and, broken-hearted, I fall in love. And just at that
time, my boy is drowned. Here, just here, in this dam.
And so what do I do? Run off and away as far as I could,
wanting not to come back, never to see this place again.
But the pain comes with me – it's always here. And the
man follows me, won't leave me alone – as drunk as my
husband and twice as demanding. I squander my money,
we live like fools. But then he gets ill, he needs the sun, so I
buy a villa near Menton, where I nurse him day and night,
night and day for three whole years. No rest, no rest and
he bleeds me dry. Debts up to here. So then I'm forced to
sell the villa, and it's back to Paris, solvent for once. And
then, guess what? Another woman. He steals all my money
and moves in with her – and there I am, quite alone.

LEKO: (*Under his breath.*) Sematla [i.e.: good for nothing]!

LULU: I tried to kill myself, you know? Shameful, utterly
stupid. But it brought me to my senses and I began to feel a
great longing for Africa, for my home, for my children. No
more punishments, Lord, please! I've paid my dues. (*She
takes a letter from her bag.*) Here's another one today. He's
asking my forgiveness, swears he can't go on without me,

would I please come back to Paris? (*Listens.*) Sounds like music. Can that be music?

LEO: Squatter kids – little skollies...

LULU: We should invite them over to play – throw a party.

LEKO sings quietly and sadly the Abba song 'Money, Money, Money'.

LULU: Not so funny, though, to be poor in a rich man's world. Perhaps we better get used to it.

LEKO: You don't have to – I've told you how.

LULU: Darling Marietjie insists on saving electricity, so we watch that ghastly television in the pitch dark – all drivel. I even miss French TV and that's saying something.

LEKO: It's the only pleasure for most people, drivel or not.

LULU: I wonder if one day we'll look back at this time and think that we dreamed it? Our *annus mirabilis* – such hope, such euphoria. But how the rainbow is fading, how corrupt people are...

LEKO: Oh, and who taught us about 'corrupt' I'd like to know? The old bunch was rotted with it.

LULU: True.

LEKO: My father never had a TV – never had a thing. Laboured all his life – no education, no chance of an ounce of dignity. Just took his anger out on me...

LULU: Ah, that thin little boy with the bloody nose...

LEKO: 'Boy'. Just so, that's what I was when I met you. Life is all chance, isn't it?

LULU: It is, it is. And now my world is upside down and yours is right side up.

LEO: I think I fell for you, Lulu, yes I think I did. In another world, who knows...?

LULU: Silly, I was far too old for you, Leko, and always will be. You need a wife now, my friend – a younger one. You've got everything but.

LEKO: True.

LEO is snoozing in a deckchair, his dark glasses on. LULU tips up the cocktail shaker and nothing comes out.

LULU: He's finished the lot the little sot. So how's about our Maria, then? She's a good girl.

LEKO: Yes.

LULU: God, when I think what she's had to cope with! Her mother was gone the next mornig poor little thing. So Johan brought the baby to me, put her in my arms and said: 'She's ours now.' Just like that. What a sweet little bundle she was, but oh, the scandal! Her mother was called Maria – we gave her the same name. She was a Sotho, like you, Leko.

LEKO: I know.

LULU: So what could I do but love her like my own? And then, when Anna arrived, they grew up like – like Juno's swans. Really, she was a gift. So you see you share a bloodline, Leko.

LEKO: Not quite. Her father…

LULU: 'Was white' you would say? Oh yes, but a good man and a brave.

LEKO: The best.

LULU: I seem doomed to philanderers, don't I? God, what this country has done to us all! Does her colour matter, I ask you? No, no and no! She's ready for another life – she's modest, she's efficient – and you like her well enough, don't you?

LEKO: She's a good girl…

LULU: … But?

LULU: (*Pause.*) Do you care about her colour? Do you?

LEO wakes up.

LEO: A job's come up, did I tell you? Only four thousand rand a month, mind you. With a bank.

LULU: You in a bank? That's pretty rich! You just stay as you are.

She falls back on the rug, laughing. Enter PUTSWA with a coat.

PUTSWA: Mr Leo, put this on please – the damp will come.

LEO: Nag, nag…

He gets up, however, and puts the coat over his shoulders. Sits in his deckchair again.

PUTSWA: Hanyane, hanyane, Mr Leo. You went off this morning and never told old Putswa.

LULU: Oh, my old Putswa, how you've aged.

PUTSWA: What can Putswa do for the madam?

LEKO: A re o tsofetse *[i.e.: How much older you have got].*

PUTSWA: Eya, I have lived a long time! The oubaas was trying to find me more wives even before Mr Leo was born. Everyone gets very excited, not me. I just go on with my work.

LEKO: They don't make them like him any more. Ngunu, I salute you.

PUTSWA: I say the servants belong to the masters and the masters belong to the servants. Today it's all upside down – the girls wear the trousers and the boys have no jobs. Hé la, Mr Leo put this on.

PUTSWA wraps a scarf round LEO's neck, stands behind his chair and strokes his hair tenderly.

LEO: Got an introduction to a chap who'll arrange a loan.

LEKO: Leo, you're just asking for trouble. You can't pay the interest – not now not ever.

LULU: Ignore it. There isn't such a chap.

A football bounces on to the stage. ANNA and PITSO run on, followed by MARIA, knitting.

LEO: Ah, the children!

ANNA: Ah, the sundowners!

LULU: Come. Come here, you two. Come sit by your ma. How much I love the both of you, my girls, you'll never know how much.

LEKO: I see our wandering radical is a bit of a ladykiller.

PITSO: Get off my case, Masopha.

LEKO: Grey hairs and still a student?

PITSO: Very funny – at least I've earned them.

LEKO: Losing our cool are we, Professor Politics?

PITSO: And what did you do for the Struggle, Mr Wheeler-Dealer?

LEKO: What d'you think I did, twiddle my thumbs? Ok, then, what do you make of me exactly?

PITSO: You're a mystery to me – the car, the gear, the fat-cat air. How did you do it? You're black but you're white. Frankly, I don't know where you stand.

LEKO: You're behind the times bra' – money doesn't equal white any more. Where've you been?

ANNA: Moscow, actually.

LEKO: Making bombs, was it, or surveillance?

PITSO: A bit of both, if you want to know.

MARIA: (*Nervous.*) No, go on about the planets, Pitso.

PITSO: Ah yes – black holes and white dwarfs.

Uncomfortable laughter.

LEO: The whole country's a black hole, now we've got democracy.

ANNA: Uncle Leo, you're the pits! You make it sound like a disease.

LULU: No, let's go on with yesterday's discussion.

PITSO: Remind me, what was that?

LEO: Pride. It was about pride.

PITSO: We didn't get very far, if I recall. Objectively, there's not all that much to be proud of, is there? Man has a brilliant brain, but as to his humanity.

ANNA: … uBuntu.

PITSO: Right, Anna! – draw a veil. The vast majority in the world still lives in squalor and unhappiness. There's work to be done on that front.

LEO: Still, death get us all in the end.

PITSO: No one really understands death – why it happens. Maybe man has a hundred senses and with death only the five we know about perish – and the other ninety-five live on.

ANNA: Maybe they live on as the ancestors?

LEKO: Oh, very African, Anna. (*Beat.*) Anyhow, science will soon tell us everything.

PITSO: Science has most of the answers, but not all – not the mysteries – but one day even those may be clear. Politics, though, that's in our grasp. Leo's not wrong, that old virus of democracy seems to have had a field day – first Russia, then us. And lo! the phoenix of freedom rises up and beats its wings…

LEO: How poetical! Don't be fooled, however, it's money that forces change, not airy-fairy ideals.

ANNA: Old cynic!

PITSO: And now we're busy fashioning the sweetest constitution ever made – checks and balances throughout, individual rights supreme – the envy of the world! Bet you didn't know that!

LEO: Fancy…

LULU: Oh, Leo, you old party pooper.

PITSO: But, big 'but', even so, there are too many whites who are chary of change. Does your DNA have an extra gene, you whites, a racist gene?

ANNA: Hey, Pietie, hang on – you know that's crap.

LEO: A universal affliction… power corrupts, you'll see.

PITSO: Everything has changed here and yet nothing has changed. Liberation has come, but the real revolution hasn't even begun!

LEKO: Give it time…

ANNA: Well, I think it's amazing – for forty-four years the Nats grabbed everything for only five million people, and now those same resources belong to forty million. To us all! Of course the butter is spread thinner!

PITSO: Just don't say the word 'miracle'.

ANNA: It bloody well is! No civil war? That's a miracle. So there!

PITSO: Look, we blacks crave the education we were denied – and the whites? Nothing, they crave nothing. If they read at all, they read trash; their science is half digested, the arts they ignore. Philistines to a man, but how they like to moan: 'Culture? What "culture"? When's the next plane out?' I can just hear them round their dinner tables, with their oh so po-faces on. I tell you, they bolt their doors to the real world, while in their own backyards vast numbers of people still struggle for every crumb. They squat in tin townships, they're crammed into hovels – no food, no heat. It's degrading, it hurts me!

LULU: Pieter, Pieter, fire-eater!

PITSO: And just look at us – us in this little island of live-and-let-die – we divert ourselves with talk…

ANNA: You're doing the talking – I want a swim.

PITSO: … just like the worst of those moaning liberals.

LEKO: 'White noise', we call it.

Laughter.

LEO: Well, foreign investment's all ready to go, if that blasted black crime would calm down.

ANNA: So the poor get the blame, like that silly refrain – and in spite of affirmative action?

LEO: Some might say 'because of'.

PITSO: Oh, yeah – apartheid is dead, so long live apartheid. Look, until you all realise the cake must be shared, we won't find the end of that Rainbow.

LEKO: No jobs, ever more murderous crime – I'm afraid investment is the answer.

PITSO: No, education is the answer! Oh, there's so much to be done – better to stop talking and just get the hell on with it.

LEKO: When I can't sleep I go walking in the dark – we're blessed with these horizons, this veld, these kranse, these skies, and living in such a country, we should really be giants, supermen…

LULU: Save them for Hollywood! The myth about a race of supermen died in Europe and now it's died here too, thank God. No talk of supermen, if you please.

KHOKOLOHO crosses U/S singing a song.

LULU: Ah, Khokoloho…

ANNA: Khokoloho…

LEO: The sun's going down, ladies and gents.

PITSO: Yes…

LEO: (*Singing quietly 'Die Stem van Suid Afrika'*)
Uit die blou van onse hemel
Uit die diepte van ons seë
Oor ons ewige gebergtes
Waar die kranse antwoord gee…

ANNA: (*To MARIA.*) God, he's embarrassing! (*They giggle.*)

LEO: It's still our national anthem – oh, all right, I'll shut up.
Always liked the tune.

ANNA: (*To MARIA.*) What tune?

*A silence. Everyone is sitting deep in thought. The turning head of the
wind pump stops still. LULU shifts uneasily. Suddenly there is a sound
in the distance, as of a breaking string, which gradually dies away.*

LULU: What was that?

LEKO: I don't know. A rockfall deep in the mines, or a lift
cable snapping – but far away.

LEO: Maybe a bird? A buzzard catching its prey?

PITSO: Hey! A UFO has landed!

LULU: Unpleasant, somehow.

Pause.

PUTSWA: I could tell the disaster was coming; a leopard
coughed and the phone wires kept humming like this…
(*He makes the sound.*)

LEO: What disaster?

PUTSWA: The Freedom.

PITSO: (*Quietly.*) Oh, my God.

Pause.

LULU: Look here, my friends, we must move, it's getting dark.

PITSO: Now, what's this?

LEO: Hah!

A STRANGER has appeared; somewhat drunk.

STRANGER: Eskies asseblief, meneer, is ek op pad na die stasie?

LEKO: He wants the road to Bethlehem. (*Giggles from the girls.*)

LEO: This is private property, old boy. No stations round here.

STRANGER: Dankie, baas, dankie. Nice evening, my baas. (*He looks at LEKO and PITSO.*) Le etsang mo le malaani? *[What are you doing here with the laanies?]* Witboeties! (*He eyes MARIA.*) And who's this fancy little hotnot cherrie, hey? (*Moves towards her.*) Give some change to a hungry man, kleinmiesies.

He holds out a begging hand; MARIA cries out, recoils.

LEKO: Hé la! Enough! Tloha mona *[Get lost]*!

LULU: Here, here, have this.

Looks in her purse; holds out a handful of coins – the STRANGER taps the bottom of her hand and the coins fall. He laughs at her shock.

LULU: Have this, here, here. (*Holds out a note, he grabs it.*)

LEKO: No, don't give him!

PITSO: Why the hell not? He needs it.

The STRANGER snatches a tin of beer from the bucket – drinks.

STRANGER: Dankie, mevrouw. (*Sidles closer to MARIA.*) Sal die kleinmiesies iets vir my gee?

He surreptitiously flicks her breast; she screams, runs to LULU.

LEKO: Voetsak, ek sê! Loop! Tsamaya! (*Threatens him off.*)

Exit the STRANGER – laughing.

LULU: Come, friends, time to go. (*Her arm around MARIA.*) Marietjie, my pet, cheer up, I think I hear wedding bells ringing.

MARIA: It's nothing to joke about, Ma – please!

As she passes LEKO, he suddenly makes a gesture with an arm flung out and drops to one knee.

LEKO: 'Oh Ophelia! Remember me in thy – er – horizons!'

MARIA is rooted to the spot, staring at him.

LULU: (*Quietly, to LEO.*) Is that quite right?

LEO: A bit off I think… somewhere.

LULU: Nearly suppertime, come along people.

They start leaving; LULU takes MARIA's arm.

MARIA: My heart's still going like the clappers.

LEKO: Mark this in your diaries, ladies and gentlemen, on the twenty-second of February the axe falls. (*Groans.*) Or not. Just bear it in mind.

Exit ALL. ANNA and PITSO remain.

ANNA: Well whew! Alone at last, as they say in the movies. Thanks to that nasty old dronkie.

PITSO: What's her problem – Maria? Is she scared I might tear the clothes off your back or what? I tell you, Anna, we are way above that stuff. See that star, the bright one burning a hole in the sky? That's what we must aim at, you and I. Look, it blazes alone, yet belongs to the others. We must be free to do that.

ANNA: You talk so well. (*Pause.*) What have you done to me, Pitso? The cherry orchard, the house, I don't seem to love them so much as I always did. This was the best place on earth for me, but now…

PITSO: Africa is your orchard, Anna – the world. The earth is vast and beautiful, full of marvellous places. (*Pause.*) Anna, think for a moment – think about your people. Oh, Anna – to *own* human beings? They'd no right to do that.

ANNA: No right, no right…

PITSO: Behind every tree in your orchard, behind every branch, every leaf, eyes are watching you. Don't you hear their voices, feel their pain? Even your mother, and maybe you yourself, can't see that you've lived off other people all your lives. Hey, no tears. We're not a normal society yet. We've been abused for centuries and crippled for fifty – there's a lot of catching up to do. If the old ones can't take the change, too bad. But we young ones must get on with the job. Madiba is right – no retribution, no revenge, just bloody hard work. That's what I'm trying to do. Are you with me, Anna?

ANNA: D'you know, Pitso, when you were teaching things to Gerrie, I used to watch you and I envied him. You were a little pair, you two. And when I went up to Wits I saw that all these years I'd felt bad about the way we lived, deurmekaar *[alternative: rackety]* as it is. I guess I needed to get away to see it clearly. I sort of know this place is not really ours any more, and so – I shall leave. I'm ready.

PITSO: Yo, yo, yo, Anna! You've unlocked your heart – now chuck away the keys. You're free as air!

ANNA: It's a bit scary.

PITSO: Anna, I've been scared too, sometimes. I've been angry and alone in strange places, like that poor drunk bastard. And yet all the time over there, deep in my heart, I felt hope. I knew it would all come right and look, it has – it will.

ANNA: The moon's coming up.

MARIA's voice is heard calling: 'Anna, where are you?'

PITSO: I feel good, Anna. I feel anything is possible now, with the two of us.

They kiss gently just as MARIA's voice calls again. They start laughing and tumble apart.

ANNA: 'Above all that stuff', eh?

He laughs, takes her face in his hands.

PITSO: Maria will hate this. D'you think your mother will too?

ANNA: She doesn't *see* colour – in this country that's a blind spot. She loves Maria, she'll love you too.

PITSO: Nobody doesn't see colour.

ANNA: You wanna bet?

She gently takes his head and they kiss for real. MARIA's voice is heard again.

PITSO: Wow, she's persistent!

ANNA: Come on, let's verneuk her, we'll go back along the river bed.

PITSO: Great, let's go.

They run off past the wind pump, hand in hand.

End of Act Two.

Act Three

The night of 22 February – moonlit, still. We look on to the covered veranda from the inside of the house, as it were, looking out towards the garden. The remnants of a braaivleis glow behind the balustrade; a white bougainvillea in full flower climbs up one of the pillars. Assorted garden chairs surround two round tables, candles lit on each. A table with drinks and food near the kitchen door UL. The door to the billiard room is UR. Buck trophies are mounted along the architrave of the veranda roof. Centre Stage steps lead down into the garden and dance area from where loud music (from the band we heard in Act Two.) is playing.

PITSO is perched on the balustrade, reading. Enter DIKELDI from the garden with a tray, followed by KHOKOLOHO who tries to flirt with her, which she won't have. ANNA comes from the dancing to fetch PITSO; he demurs. LULU dances on with a reluctant MARIA. PIK follows them and flops, exhausted, into a cane chair. PUTSWA Enters from the kitchen with a tray of fresh drinks. Exit ALL except PICKETT and PITSO.

PIK: (*Yells above the music.*) Thank you, Putswa! (*PUTSWA goes.*)
Shouldn't be doing this, y'know. (*To PITSO.*) Specially not this boom-boom stuff. Blood pressure's not ace; had a little heart thing a few years back, but what the hell. I've gotta lotta bark but not much bite left, as they say. Strong as a horse, though. My late father used to say the family was descended from the very horse Caligula shoved into the Senate. He liked his little jokes, my old man. 'Shmincitatus' I say – a racehorse would've been more use than a bloody Senator; we might have made some sodding money, my lot. Heigh-ho, the hungry dog dreams only of a bone.
(*Drops off, then wakes with shouts from the billiard room where NYATSO and KHOKOLOHO are playing.*)

Enter KELE – bops on the stoep, gazing out to the dancing.

PITSO: Now you mention it, I can see horse in you.

PIK: Ah. Well. Your horse is a fine animal. You can make money from a horse.

Enter MARIA from the dancing, with a tray of used plates. Exit DIKELEDI rushing back guiltily into the kitchen.

PITSO: Madam Masopha Lebaka herself!

MARIA: (*To PIK.*) She hired the band, can you believe – and how do we pay them, I'd like to know?

Exit MARIA, furious, to the kitchen with her tray.

PIK: Me and dogs – I dream money all the time.

PITSO: Money, money, money! What's the *point* of your life?

PIK: German philosopher-type – what's his name? Sounds like 'niks nie'. *[i.e.: 'nothing' in Afrikaans]*

PITSO: Nietzsche?

PIK: That's the one – great mind – incredibly famous…

PITSO: Fascist…

PIK: … says it's quite all right to forge banknotes.

PITSO: And have you read Nietzsche?

PIK: Well, no, but Daphne has. Wouldn't mind having a shot meself; got to find five grand by tomorrow and… (*Pats his pocket, stands in alarm.*) Jeezuz, it's gone!

Runs off into the garden yelling 'Nobody leave!', bumping into LULU and KARLOTTA who Enter from the garden.

LULU: Why's Leo so damned late? (*Calls through the kitchen door.*) Kele, check the boys are all right for drinks, would you? (*V/O* 'Yes, Miss Lulu!.*)

PITSO: Maybe the auction didn't happen.

LULU: Oh, pooh!

Re-enter PICKETT.

PIK: Found it – dropped into the lining – big hole – Daphne's shirking.

LULU: This is absolutely not the moment for a party. Oh well, fiddle while Rome burns. (*Sits with a cool drink.*)

KARLOTTA suddenly sings out 'da-daah!' and breaks into the can-can, while ANNA and MARIA are her back-up team from the balustrade. KHOKOLOHO and NYATSO Enter from the billiard room to watch. Everybody cheers wildly at each trick. She does a thing with an exploding rose, then pulls a paper streamer from KHOKOLOHO's ear.

KHOKO: Hé la, boloyi, metlhoho… shu *[i.e.: witchcraft, wonders]*!

KARLOTTA: Pick a card, Pik. Quick!

PIK: Right, I have.

KARLOTTA: Einstein. Now cut the pack. Goed. Hand me back, meneer, the little pack. Een, twee, drie! What card did you pick?

PIK: The eight of spades.

KARLOTTA: So look in your top pocket and tell me what you find.

He finds the card in his top pocket and holds it up for all to see. It's the eight of spades; cheers from everyone.

KARLOTTA: Da-daah! (*Reshuffles and turns to PITSO.*) Quick, professor, guess at the top card, please.

PITSO: Er… the queen of spades.

KARLOTTA: (*Shows it.*) Bakgat! (*To PIK.*) The top card please, again.

PIK: The ace of hearts.

She's got the wrong card so she pockets the pack quickly and bluffs.

KARLOTTA: Keerect again! (*Sits next to PIK and turns his head like a ventriloquist's dummy.*) What a beautiful evening we're having. *[Voice: Ja-nee, liewe Lottie, beautiful.]* What a handsome chap you are! *[Voice: You're not so bad yourself.]*

PIK: Lottie the ventriloquist, hey? There's no end to your talents. You quite pluck the heartstrings, old girl.

KARLOTTA: You still got one? (*Lays her ear to his chest.*) Hah – strong like a horse!

PIK: (*Sings.*) 'I've got you under my skin – I've got you deep in the heart of me…'

KARLOTTA: Hy's 'n goeie mens maar 'n slegte musikant.

Laughter from everyone.

KARLOTTA: Aandag asseblief! The last, the very last final trick! Dames en here, what do we have here? (*Whips a car rug off a chair and backs up to the steps.*) A rug and a rug and a very fine rug. Any takers for a top-class rug? (*An Indian-Arab shimmy, and two arms and a leg appear, Shiva-like, from behind the rug.*) Een! Twee! Drie!

She flourishes the rug to one side and ANNA is revealed, who goes 'Da-daah!' and runs to kiss her mother. Applause etc.

LULU: And for the very last time, dames en here… eentweedrie!

Swish of rug and MARIA bows shly. Applause.

PIK: Think what I've been missing all these years!

KARLOTTA: *Voilà!* The End! Bonsewer monsewer. (*Throws the rug over PIK and runs off into the garden.*)

PIK: Hey, hey, you! I'm coming after you, you wicked creature!

Gallops after her. Exit BOTH.

LULU: Still no Leo, what's he *doing* in town so long? Drinking himself to death, I shouldn't wonder…

MARIA: Ma, Uncle has bought it, for sure.

PITSO: You wish!

LULU: Ah, but, she set a ceiling to her bounty, but one musn't look a gift-horse in the mouth, must one? Lady Luck is throwing her dice tonight – oh, my heart…

PITSO: So there, little Mrs Alexander Know-All!

MARIA: Mr Know-All yourself! The only man to be thrown out of the same university twice.

PITSO: Not thrown out. Left. Two universities. Once.

LULU: No need to get so cross, Marietjie. So what if he teases you about Leko? We'd all like you to marry him; he's practically family already. But if not, not. Nobody, darling is forcing you.

MARIA: Yes-no, I know…

LULU: Go on, marry him – why wait?

MARIA: Darling Ma, I can hardly propose to him myself, can I? Everyone goes, 'blah blah blah will she, won't she?' But he makes terrible jokes or goes silent on me. 'S'OK – I can see why, he's too busy with his affairs to notice me, but I wish, *I wish*, I had my own money, and then, boy! – you wouldn't see me for dust. I'd be a nursing sister, a remedial teacher – I don't know – something *useful.*

PITSO: Very commendable, I approve.

MARIA: And I don't need your approval, thanks! Or your smartass sarcasm. It's just that I can't stand doing nothing, Ma, I *must* have things to do!

A sharp crack and shouts of laughter from the billiard room. Enter NYATSO trying to hide his glee.

NYATSO: Khokoloho's bust the billiard cue!

Exit NYATSO.

MARIA: And who said Khokoloho could play? Who said he could come inside? Honestly!

She storms off to investigate. Exit MARIA.

LULU: You're naughty to tease her, Pietertjie, she's a sensitive little plant.

KHOKOLOHO tiptoes across the back to the kitchen.

PITSO: And why shouldn't Khokoloho play if he wants to?
She meddles in everything, she follows us around like she's
scared of a romance or something stupid like that. Anna
and me have many things besides 'love' to discuss. We're
way above it.

LULU: I'm not all that sure that I am. (*Agitated.*) Where's that
Leo? Sold or not sold? I don't know what to think. I'm lost.
Tell me anything, something. Speak to me…

PITSO: Come, calm yourself, Mrs R. Close this book and open
a fresh one – no more white nostalgia. For once in your
life, you're going to have to look truth straight in the eye.

LULU: Oh, fine. But what truth, pray? You with your young
eyes can see truth and untruth but I have lost my vision.
You can look boldly ahead, Pitso, because the future's all
yours. I see a void. Accidents of history, that's all we are;
you should take pity on us poor 'laanies', you heartless
boy. I was born here, Anna was too. Mother and Father
lived here all their lives, Great-Grandfather built it and
I love this house – I just can't imagine my life without it,
without the cherry orchard. Sell it, sell me. This is the place
my son was drowned, Pitso. Don't be too hard.

PITSO: Not hard – realistic. The land was up for grabs. You
grabbed. That's history. Now another thing must happen.

LULU: But it's still so hard to take.

PITSO: I sympathise, Mrs R, really I do.

*She takes out her handkerchief and a letter falls out, which he picks
up.*

LULU: My heart feels like lead today, all this noise… but I'm
scared of silence. Pitso, I love you like my – like a son.
Always wanted you to do well – we both did. If you and
Anna marry – and don't think for a moment I haven't
seen the love-light in my daughter's eyes – I shall be truly
happy. You see, my little fighter, things are not all bad in
our new SA are they? Dear Pietie, you've been thrown
around from pillar to post, but now you must study.

PITSO: I am, I am…

LULU: Mama always said to me: 'Finish what you started' and now I say it to you. I'm not wrong, am I? (*She touches his cheek fondly.*) Ha, you need a shave!

PITSO: I'm no pin-up I admit, take me or leave me.

She spies the letter in his hand and, relieved, takes it back.

LULU: They never stop coming. The wild man is ill again, in trouble again, the same old song. He's ill, he misses me, he's miserable, and who'll remember to feed him his pills at the right hour? You disapprove? But what am I to do? He haunts me, why hide it? I love the bastard, obviously. There, it's out! I love him, love him, love him! He drags me down, he drives me mad and I'll probably go to hell with him, but I can't live without him. Don't say a word, Pieterjie, not a word, it won't help.

PITSO: The guy cheated on you, didn't he?

LULU: Say nothing. Not a word. It's no good.

PITSO: The guy's a bastard. Look what he's done to you.

LULU: You know nothing about what love does. You should by now – you're old enough.

PITSO: But he's not worth it, he's just a shit.

LULU: And don't give me this 'I'm above it' stuff – I detest jargon. Even radicals are allowed to fall in love, you know.

PITSO: What are you saying? Anna and me…

LULU: And high time, too. Nearly thirty and still not married? Not even a mistress? Are you a prude? Are you…? I mean, it's not quite – I don't know – normal is it?

PITSO: What did you say? What are you trying to say? I don't believe my ears! (*He rushes off but comes right back.*) That is it between us! That's it!

Exit PITSO into the garden. She calls after him.

LULU: Pitso! Wait! I was only joking, it was a joke! Come back!

From O/S the sounds of shrieks and laughter.

LULU: Ohmygod, what's happened?

Enter ANNA followed by NYATSO, both doubled up with laughter.

ANNA: Pitso fell into the ha-ha!

Exit ANNA.

LULU: Funny fellow, he is.

ANNA and MARIA, giggling, bring in a reluctant PITSO.

LULU: Oh, dear Pitso, dear dear Pitso, I apologise, truly, really. Dance with me? Please?

PITSO: Gays don't dance with girls.

Everybody explodes again.

ANNA: You shouldn't take it as an insult, Pietie, honestly.

LULU: Pietertjie, it's so far from the truth, you must know I was teasing. I ask forgiveness. Will you dance with me?

Sulkily he lets her take his hand and they leave. Enter PUTSWA with his stick.

NYATSO: What's up, ngunu?

PUTSWA: I don't feel good. Once upon a time judges, professors, surgeons would come to our parties. But now we send for a band of tsotsis from the location. My old master, the father of mosadinyana, used to give me bicarb of soda in warm water every morning, sick or not sick. Just like him. For sixty years I drink it and that is why I'm still living.

NYATSO: You should go back to dithakong – the place of your birth – and live your days in peace. You have worked enough.

PUTSWA: Hayi suka! This is my home. Ha-ana maitseo *[i.e.: He has no manners]*!

Enter LULU and PITSO from the garden.

LULU: *Merci*, I'll call it a day, Pitso. I must sit if you don't mind.

Enter ANNA at a run.

ANNA: A man came to the kitchen to say the cherry orchard was sold!

LULU: My God! Who to?

ANNA: He wouldn't say. He's gone.

ANNA pulls PITSO away to the billiard room.

NYATSO: Only rumours, madame. Some ouk, a stranger.

PUTSWA: And Mr Leo is wearing the wrong jacket, he'll catch cold. Oupa would say, 'Bicarb for you, m'boy!'

LULU: Quick, Nyatso, run after him, find out who.

NYATSO: The guy's gone. (*Laughs.*)

LULU: What's tickled you, Nyatso?

NYATSO: Sorry, madame – Khokoloho's such a clown. Parathlathlé!

LULU: Putswa, old fellow, if the house is sold, where will you go?

PUTSWA: Where you tell me to go, my mosadinyana, that's where I'll go.

LULU: You don't look right. Are you quite well? Why not go to bed.

PUTSWA: Eya… (*He grins.*) I go to bed and who keeps his eye on everybody – who attends to everything? There's only me now for the whole house.

PUTSWA sits in a chair near the kitchen door, grumbling.

NYATSO: Please, Mrs Rademeyer, please, I must ask you a big favour. If you go to Paris again, take me with you. I cannot, I *cannot* stay here. The food is disgusting – there's nothing to do. My life has changed. These are my people, but I

THE FREE STATE: ACT THREE

don't want to be with them any more. I must go with you
– please!

PICKETT gallops on.

PIK: May I ask you, my beauty, for a dance? (*She gets up
wearily.*) I must take some money off you, enchanting Lucy,
a mere trifle…

Exit LULU and PIK. Enter KELE from the garden.

KELE: My head's up there… dancing, dancing, dancing. Ntate,
one of the band boys just told me something which made
me lose my breath.

PUTSWA: What did the tsotsi say to you, huh?

KELE: Your eyes, he said, shine like a sweet young baby calf.

PUTSWA clicks his tongue in disapproval.

NYATSO: Oh, *dis donc!*

Exit NYATSO into the garden.

KELE: I wish *he'd* say poetry to me.

PUTSWA: Young girls should only listen to the man they will
marry.

*Enter KHOKOLOHO, thunderous, who grabs KELE's arm and sweeps
her D/S.*

KHOKO: You keep away from me, Dikeledi. You look right
through me, like I was an insect. You make my life a lousy
thing. Why?

DIKELDI: Khokoloho, that hurts! (*She breaks away from his grip
and sits.*) So what d'you want from me?

KHOKO: You've put me in a muddle – this way, that way – I
don't know how to be. I look at the world with a smile
on my face, but inside I'm crying sometimes. Maybe I do
things wrong, but my heart is not wrong – my heart knows
you are for me.

KELE: Khokoloho, this is not the place to have such a talk. We can talk later, but not now. I have things to think about, so please leave me, dhu!

KHOKO: Every time a disaster. But look, Parathlathlé can smile – he can even laugh. Listen! Ha-ha!

Enter MARIA hearing his rather wild laughter.

MARIA: Making scenes in public, Khokoloho – have you no shame? Off you go, Dikeledi, there's washing up to be done.

Exit KELE.

MARIA: Khokoloho, first you play billiards, which you have no right to do, and then you go and bust a cue of Mr Leo's!

KHOKO: Ha-ha!

MARIA: He'll be very upset, I can tell you. And now here you are lounging about as if you were one of the guests!

KHOKO: Excuse me, *Miss* Maria, but you have no right to tell me things like this.

MARIA: Why we employ you I just don't know.

KHOKO: Hé la! I work in the day; at night I do what I like, and only my elders can say that I must not do this and I must not do that, not you. Who are you? You're not black and you're not white. What are you? Maybe nothing, I say!

MARIA: I don't believe my ears! What did you say?

KHOKO: Hey, hey, hey, OK, OK. We both say strong things…

MARIA: This is my father's house! Out of here! Get out of here this instant! (*Chases him round the tables.*) Out of my sight! Out! Out!

She grabs PUTSWA's stick from his hands as he sits quietly, and chases KHOKOLOHO, who runs out to the garden and then pops back.

KHOKO: I'm going to tell about you!

MARIA: Come on then, come! I'll show you! (*She swings the stick wildly just as LEKO enters from the garden.*) You dare come back and you'll get this! Hamba!

She finds herself caught in LEKO's arms for a moment.

LEKO: That is quite a welcome

MARIA: Ha! Pardon. I beg yours.

LEKO: Not at all. An enthusiastic reception is always gratifying.

MARIA: Oh, my pleasure I'm sure. (*Gently.*) Siestog, did I get you? Did I?

LEKO: No problem. Just a small egg coming up, that's all.

Voices off: 'I just saw Leko come'/'Is Leko here by God?' etc. PICKETT Enters first.

PIK: In the flesh! About time, old chap. I smell a touch of the old elbow juice. Us too, having a fine old time…

Enter LULU.

LULU: Alexander The Great and high time too! Why so long? And where's Leo?

LEKO: No, no, he's on his way – we came together.

LULU: Well? Tell all. Did the sale happen? Tell, tell.

LEKO: (*Wary of revealing his joy.*) The sale ended three hours ago; we were the last – the cherry on the fruitcake! Hah, sorry. Some of us had to drown our sorrows as it were. My head's slightly – y'know…

Enter LEO, chewing.

LULU: Leo, Leo, here you are. Oh, for God's sake, Leo, speak!

LEO: Biltong – sorry – haven't eaten. God what a day! I'm completely bushed. Help me to change, Putswa.

Exit LEO and PUTSWA. Enter ANNA and PITSO.

LULU: (*Calling after him.*) Leo, what happened? God!

PIK: The auction, old chap? What went on?

LULU: Is the cherry orchard sold?

LEKO: It's sold.

LULU: Who bought it?

A pause.

LEKO: I bought it.

> *LULU is stunned. MARIA takes a bunch of keys from a pocket, walks towards LEKO and drops them on the floor at his feet. Exit MARIA. Enter KARLOTTA, KHOKOLOHO, NYATSO and KELE, variously, to listen.*

LEKO: I bought it! Just a sec, ladies and gentlemen – don't know if I can put my words together. Wessels is there looking like a cat that got the cream and I just know I have to wipe that smile. Once Leo is out of it, I just have to wipe that smile. He starts going up in fives, so me, I raise him ten every time. And it's war! Well, at last it's finished. I go a million over his last bid of 900,000 and it's mine! He can't go any more, see? The smile is wiped! Bang on a million and the cherry orchard is mine, all mine!

He laughs – he holds his arms wide, embracing the air round LULU.

LEKO: The house is mine, the land is mine – could it be that you are mine? I'm not drunk, I'm not sleep-walking, I'm not out of my mind… (*He lifts and stamps his feet in African dance mode, jubilant.*) My ancestors will see what I have done; they will rise from their graves and see how their son – little Masopha with the snotty nose, who could hardly add two and two, who ran kaalvoet in winter, who was always hungry – that same little Masopha now owns this land, the finest thing in the whole wide world! (*He runs down the steps and takes a fistful of earth from the flower beds – returns holding it high.*) Eh, now my people can rest, the land is back where it has to be. Did it happen? Do I dream it? No, look, she dropped these at my feet because now she knows who runs the show. (*He picks up the keys.*) Well, so it is. Hey, bashimane, let's hear some music! Now, my friends, you'll see how Masopha Lebaka takes his axe and chops those trees, how that orchard falls down one by one! Pah-papah!

He mimes the axe. A cry from LULU; ANNA stands behind her mother glaring at LEKO.

LEKO: We'll build the weekend pondoks and we'll build a fine new township, and our children and their children's children will live a whole new life here! Hey, there – music! Mpapaleng! Bapalang mino *[i.e.: play music]*!

Music. KHOKOLOHO, KELE, and NYATSO leave for the garden. LULU is crying bitterly. LEKO kneels beside her.

LEKO: Why oh why did you not listen to me? My poor good Lucy, you cannot bring it back with these. What was mine is now mine again – it's simple and it's also hard, I know, I know. But this moment will pass.

PIK: Let her cry. Come outside and let her be for a bit. Come.

LEKO: Hey, skollies! Play 'Shosholoza'! Special request from the brand new baas! Watch out for the Madiba of the Cherry Orchard! Viva Lebaka! (*He bumps into a table, which falls over.*) No worries – money's no object.

Exit LEKO and PIK to the garden. Exit KARLOTTA into the house.

'Shosholoza' is sung from the garden. LULU, weeping, crawls across to the table to set it to rights. ANNA goes to her mother and kneels beside her, taking her in her arms. PITSO quietly leaves for the garden.

ANNA: Mother, sweet Mother, oh don't cry. Dear, kind, darling Ma, I love you Ma, I really do. Yes, the orchard is gone, that's true. It's true, but don't cry, Ma, there's still a life ahead for you. And maybe, just maybe, it's meant. And maybe it was never really ours and it does truly belong to Leko, and to Pitso, and to Putswa. We can plant another, hey? – even lovelier than this, and you can see it grow, and you'll understand and a quiet, deep happiness will come to you, like at sunset. Now let's see that smile, Ma, Mommy, Mama? Come?

She helps her mother off through the billiard room door. Sheet lighting in the distance and faint rumbles of thunder. A gust of wind rustles the bougainvillea.

End of Act Three.

Act Four

End of March; late afternoon.

Back to the 'nursery'. The bookshelves stand empty, the furniture and carpets are gone. There are four tea chests standing around, full of books. Pale rectangles on the walls where the pictures used to hang. The portrait of Johan is draped, leaning against a bookcase on the floor. It is raining outside; huge cracks of thunder and lightning begin the Act. The shutters are wide open to a dark sky.

A hum of voices off; people have come to take their leave. LEO's voice is heard saying: 'Thanks, friends, we thank you all, stay well my friends' etc.

LEKO stands waiting in the room holding a plastic bag. NYATSO spruces up champagne glasses with a cloth and places them on a tray balanced on a tea chest.

NYATSO: It's like the whole township is saying goodbye. Bhari!

LEKO: You open this. (*Handing him a bottle of champagne.*)

NYATSO: Good hearts, no brains.

LEKO: You talk of your mother like that? Ha-una tlhompo *[i.e.: You have no respect]*!

Enter LULU and LEO.

LEO: You can't do that, Luly old girl – empty your purse to those people like that, you just can't!

LULU: Well, there you go, it's done. It can't be helped. It's done.

Exit LULU and LEO.

LEKO: (*Follows after them.*) Hello? Champagne? I've bought you some champagne. A farewell glass between us? No? (*Returns.*) They only had one bottle left in the hotel bar. 'Net een botteltjie vir die tjaffer', nê? (*NYATSO giggles.*) But that should do us, I don't touch the stuff. (*Back to the door.*) No takers? Well, you have some, Nyatso.

NYATSO: This isn't the real thing, I can tell you.

LEKO: South Africa's finest – you'll have to live with it.

NYATSO: To those who're going and to those who are staying behind, poor bastards. *Santé.*

LEKO: What's so funny?

NYATSO: I'm leaving, I'm happy.

LEKO: Your mother won't be; u hloka tlhompo! Damn this rain, it's holding me up. (*Calling out through the door.*) Dames en here, the plane goes at eight ten – we must leave in twenty minutes, latest.

Enter PITSO shaking out a wet jacket.

PITSO: Time to go. (*Calling through her door.*) Anna, did you see my hat? Can't find it.

LEKO: Only another month to go and it'll be ideal weather for building. Can't wait. These hands of mine – bloody things just flap about like they don't belong to me.

PITSO: We'll be gone soon and then you can blow the place up if you want.

LEKO: (*A hoot of laughter.*) 'Zactly what I'm going to do! But not a word to them will you? I'd never sell this house with weekenders on the doorstep. D'you like this stuff? (*Offering champagne.*)

PITSO: Do me a favour.

LEKO: So – nose to the grindstone, is it?

PITSO: Yup – down to Fort Hare to collect my papers and then back up to Wits with Anna. My prof's moved up there.

LEKO: And the flag's will be out – the mighty Struggle Hero, huh?

PITSO: Dead funny.

LEKO: A chap like you should be in business; got a good head on you. You've studied enough.

PITSO: All your talk about building weekend hideaways for the tired businessman. Shu! Holidays are for laanies – you don't get holidays until you get jobs. Where are you? On Mars?

LEKO: No, OK, Pitso, hold it, hold it. Of course I'm with you – the RDP takes precedence. I'm giving first refusal to the local authority, you know, in case they want the land for their housing programme.

PITSO: (*Still suspicious.*) Viva.

LEKO: If they do, I'll put in for the contracts, see, and build ten houses where there might just have been one. Neat, hey? Lay on water, electricity – the works.

PITSO: Kwa-Masophaville, hey? Look, bra', I don't object to profit per se, because sure as hell the country needs risk - takers, but first things first, the homeless must be housed. Still, I take off my hat to you – if I had it. (*He calls out through the door again.*) Anna! Beneath it all you're a good soul , bra'. Even if your hands do flop about.

LEKO: Ah, my hands… yes. Look here, in case you need it, here's something to smooth your way a bit.

LEKO waves a wedge of notes from his briefcase; PITSO declines.

PITSO: Don't need it, thanks. Russian speakers are in demand these days. 'My *shapka*! My *shapka*! My kingdom for my *shapka*!'

LEKO: Your what?

PITSO grins and points to his head.

PITSO: Russians are hot-heads.

MARIA: (*O/S from ANNA's room.*) Here, take the blerry thing!

A Russian fur hat comes sailing through the open door.

PITSO: Hey, why so angry? What did I do? (*Dusting it off.*) This brings back memories – her name was Varya. (*Puts it on rakishly.*) Mafia-style, heh? Khótchesh kúpit narkótiki *[Russian: You wanna buy some drugs]*?

LEKO: Who you fooling? Take the bread, man.

PITSO: It wasn't our pockets, Masopha, but our veins we emptied as we toyi-toyi'd our way to freedom.

LEKO: That's history, Pitso. Now we have to make that freedom work for us. Money helps.

PITSO: Look, we share the same beginnings, but there our ways part: you value your riches, I value my ideals. We each go our own road, that's all.

Pause. LEKO walks toward PITSO.

LEKO: I'd say our ideals are closer to each other than you appear to think.

LEKO holds out his left hand in front of PITSO's eyes, fingers up, palm towards his own face. PITSO is puzzled.

LEKO: See? While you were in Moscow, the bastards had fun with my fingernails.

PITSO is silenced. LEKO puts the money away. The rain has stopped. Brilliant sunshine breaks through the window. The sound of a chainsaw on wood is heard in the distance.

LEKO: Work is the only dignity, Pitso. When I work long hours my thoughts move easily and I seem to know why I exist. But I'm always aware that there are millions who must spend the day hoping only to see the next sunrise and that's possibly where I come in… Still, anyway, we'll call it quits.

LEKO holds out his hand and they shake, African-style.

PITSO: You devil, why didn't you say before?

LULU's voice from O/S calling, 'Anna!'

LEKO: Ah, well, the world goes on turning. Leo took that job at the bank, y'know – they hang together, these whiteys, don't they?

PITSO: The 'Leos' don't really figure any more, do they, brother?

Enter ANNA.

ANNA: Ma says to lay off the orchard till after she's left.

Exit ANNA. PITSO hugs LEKO warmly.

PITSO: Yup, a bit of tact required, bra'. Ciaou.

Exit PITSO.

LEKO: Hé lang, these young people

Exit LEKO. Re-enter ANNA, NYATSO and KHOKOLOHO.

ANNA: Has Putswa gone to hospital?

NYATSO: I know Tshepo was told to – I guess he's taken him.

ANNA: Khokoloho, check if he's gone would you?

NYATSO: Tshepo was told! Don't you believe me?

KHOKO: Ntate Putswa has no need for doctors; he should join the ancestors and I would rejoice for him. Eh. (*As he turns to go, the suitcase he is carrying springs open, spilling the contents.*) Cho cho – always the same story.

Enter KELE who helps repack; KHOKOLOHO refuses her help. Exit KHOKOLOHO with suitcase. The chainsaws stop.

NYATSO: (*Giggling to himself.*) Parathlathlé.

Enter MARIA, a letter in her hand.

MARIA: Has Putswa been taken to hospital?

ANNA: Apparently.

NYATSO: *Mais oui! Zut alors!*

MARIA: And this letter from Ma to the doctor? Why didn't they take it with him?

ANNA: Oh, damn – it'll have to be sent on to him.

ANNA takes the letter from her and Exits.

MARIA: Your mother's here, Nyatso, she wants to say goodbye.

NYATSO falls down in a mock faint. MARIA gives a scathing look and exits. KELE kneels down beside him.

KELE: Nyatso, Nyatso. You could at least look at me. Just look at me even once, Nyatso. You may never see me again. Ever.

NYATSO: Twelve more hours and I'll be in Paris again. *Vive la France!* This place isn't for me any more. I can't live here, it can't be helped, I've changed. I've just had enough. Hey, a bit of self-control, my cherrie – *enough!*

KELE: Write me a letter from Paris. Or just a postcard to say how you are. With a nice picture? My heart feels so heavy. I loved you, you know, Nyatso. Really. A lot.

Exit KELE.

NYATSO: Well, I had a good time...

Enter LULU, LEO, ANNA, then KARLOTTA carrying a dog box and bags. She sits on a tea chest.

LEO: If you want aisle seats we must go. (*Teasing NYATSO.*) M'sieur Eau de Poisson, is it? Fwah!

LULU: Another ten minutes and we'll leave. (*Looking around the room.*) Farewell, my house, dear old crippled house. They'll have you pulled down if you're not careful. Totsiens... *au revoir...* farewell lekkerlewe. Think what these walls have seen! (*Kisses her daughter.*) My dorlie, my sweetheart, you look shining, those eyes are sparkling like diamonds. Are you pleased? Very pleased?

ANNA: Ja, Ma, I am, a new life is about to begin.

LEO: Alles sal regkom, they say, and it has. All happened for the best. Amazing what a decision does – before the sale we were all nervy and anxious, and then – bingo! – it's sold and it's like a burden has been lifted and here I am, a banker. Yellow into the middle. Luly, you look better, whatever you feel.

LULU: *Merci*, Nyatso, (*He offers the tray.*) and will you check my rooms? (*He goes.*) Yes, Leo, I sleep lighter, relieved of a – you're right – a burden. My little girl, it might not be too long before I'm back – Auntie's moolah won't get very far in Paris, *c est tellement cher.* She's a godsend, our auntie, dividing up the lolly between us all. Let's drink to her, shall we?

They all make a toast to Auntie Newlands.

ANNA: Come back soon, very soon, won't you? When I've got my degree, I'll find some sort of job and you'll come to stay with us, won't you, Ma? Paris is nothing – Jo'burg's where it's at, Ma, you'll see.

LEO: What a turn-up for the books!

LULU: Oh, don't mention books, Leo. Look, it's so sad…

She's inspecting a tea chest full of the books. She sees Johan's portrait, shrouded, leaning against it. She lifts the sheet.

ANNA: I thought I could take it with me – Pitso asked if we could?

LULU: I can't think of a better home for him, sweetheart.

Enter LEKO, also NYATSO. KARLOTTA, sitting on a suitcase, has been singing 'Jan Pierewiet' to herself; the family now notice her.

LEO: (*To LEKO.*) Get Maria Callas over there.

KARLOTTA: (*She cradles a bag in her arms.*) Jou Mammie gaan weg, my kleintjie, totsiens my skatterbol. *[*The pretend baby: 'Wah! Wah!'*]* Shush, my poppie, my liewe seuntjie moet nou gaan slaap. *[*'Wah! Wah!'*]* Ag, sies! Jy het my natgemaak! I feel so blerrie sorry for you. (*She throws the baby down; speaks to LEKO.*) You'll give me a job, nê? I can't manage without.

LEKO: No problem, we'll find one for you. Shu! – life is so weird.

KARLOTTA: Thank you, geagte Meneer.

Her little dog whines and scratches in his box; she quiets it.

LEO: We're all off into the wild blue yonder. Maria's going away. Anna too. We're not needed any more.

KARLOTTA: I've got nowhere to go. Never mind.

PICKETT appears at the door, fanning himself.

PIK: Just need to catch the breath. Do we have any water, Nyatso, old chap? No, not the bubbly, I'm off it these days.

Exit NYATSO.

LEO: After more money – I'm out of here.

Exit LEO.

PIK: Not been around for yonks, lovely Lulu. (*To LEKO.*) Ah! Good to see you too – talented fellow you are. Here's for you. (*Hands him money.*) Five hundred rand – another thousand to come.

LEKO: I'm dreaming, of course. From where?

PIK: Amazing thing, some Brit mining company came prospecting round my place, found something called, let's see, molly-diddyum. No, molly-biddidum. Anyways, they call it Molly-B for short. Not oil, alas, too much to hope for, but it's a real find, they say. Aerospace stuff – NASA and so on. There's a thousand for you, amazing lady, and the rest later.

NYATSO returns with a glass of water.

PIK: Ta, it's an oven out there. Some old friend of Daphne's was going on the other day about a Chinese philosopher who advises jumping off roofs. 'Jump,' says the sage, 'and your problems are over.' No need for that now.

He pours the entire glass of water over his head and hands the glass to NYATSO.

LEKO: And the Brits…?

PIK: I've fixed a ground lease for twenty-four years, that'll see me out. Must dash. First to the Evans's, then on to the Fletchers – I owe them all. Your good health. I'll pop round on Thursday.

LULU: I'm gone by then. Today, in fact.

PIK: How's that? My God, yes – the books, the cars out front, I'm blind! Well, that's life. Useful chaps these Brits. Be happy. Is this what the Frogs do? (*Kisses LULU's hand.*) Go well. Things come to an end in this world, so if you ever hear that this has given out, remember this strange old horse and say, 'I knew him, Horatio…' Hot as hell. Daphne asks to be remembered…

Exit PIK. A pause.

LULU: Well. That's that then. Antjie, two things are nagging at me; my old Putswa…?

ANNA: Ma, he's been taken to the hospital, Tshepo saw to it earlier.

LULU: Oh, thank God! My other sadness is Maria – she's like a fish out of water with nothing to do. Leko, was I wrong to hope you might get together, you and Maria? (*To ANNA – sotto.*) Can we steal another five minutes?

She signs to ANNA who takes out KARLOTTA.

LULU: She's been fond of you since ever – she'd suit you, I think.

LEKO: Hum…

LULU: It doesn't always have to be for love, you know – children, partnership, help through this life, whatever. She's damned efficient you know, and so sweet.

LEKO: What the heck, let's go for it. (*He dives for the* Hamlet *in his briefcase, waves it at LULU.*) 'The readiness is all', hey? (*LULU laughs.*) I'd never get round to it if it weren't for you.

LULU: *Formidable!* I'll call her.

LEKO: The champagne's all ready. Hey, it's empty, someone's had the lot! (*NYATSO is chortling; LEKO shakes the empty bottle at him.*)

LULU: Nyatso, *méchant, viens!* (*Calls O/S.*) Maria, darling, drop everything and come down, would you? *Allons-y,* Nyatso.

Exit LULU and NYATSO. Muffled giggles. Enter MARIA. A pause.

MARIA: Weird. I've been looking and looking for it.

LEKO: For what?

MARIA: Perhaps it's in this. (*She rummages in a tea chest.*) I should know where, it's me that packed it.

LEKO: You're going where, exactly?

MARIA: People called Poliakov in Muizenberg, they're going overseas for a bit. I'm house-sitting for them.

She moves to the next tea chest. He stuffs back all the things she's flung out.

LEKO: The Cape, eh? Well, you'll like it there, I'd say. It's where you should be...

MARIA: (*A sharp look.*) With my own people, you mean?

LEKO: (*An evasive shrug.*) It's one helluva drive by yourself, though, will you be OK? So, it's the end of life in this house...

They talk across each other for these two speeches, while moving from tea chest to tea chest as MARIA pretends to look.

MARIA: Maybe it's in here. Ja, ja, life in this place is finished and klaar. No more ever again.

LEKO: And I'm back to Jo'burg – same plane as them. Khokoloho will be in charge here, I'm keeping him on.

MARIA: Oh, are you just? (*MARIA stops still and looks at him squarely.*)

LEKO: Was last March as hot as this? Been dry as a bone, till today. Must be in the nineties...

MARIA: No idea. Anyway our barometer is bust. Khokoloho bust it.

LEO's voice calls from O/S: 'Mr Lebaka!'

LEKO: (*As if he'd been expecting the call.*) On my way!

Exit LEKO at a run. Enter LULU, slowly.

LULU: Well? (*Pause.*) Oh, really! He's hopeless!

MARIA: (*Pulls herself together.*) No, Ma, he and me were hopeless. I'll sleep in Colesburg tonight; I'll leave when you leave.

LULU: (*Hugs MARIA fiercely.*) We have got to go, sweet. (*Calls.*) Antjie! Annie, darling!

Enter ANNA, then variously PITSO, LEO, KARLOTTA, KELE. KHOKOLOHO and NYATSO clear the tea chests.

LULU: Well, there we are. (*To ANNA.*) It's all over.

MARIA: (*A sudden smile.*) I'm, like, free.

ANNA: Viva! I'm proud of you, Marietjie. (*They both laugh, hug.*)

LEO: My family, my darling family, and – comrades. I cannot possibly say nothing, can I? But I find I cannot express the feelings which fill my whole being and I cannot bear to look at these empty... Leaving this house for the last time...

ANNA: You promised, Uncle.

LEO: Double the yellow into the middle pocket – pham!

ANNA: Pham!

LEO: I say nothing.

Enter LEKO, followed by KHOKOLOHO.

PITSO: Planes don't wait. We'll have to get weaving.

LULU: I'm seeing the walls of this house with new eyes, the ceilings even. You sort of take them for granted. I'll miss every corner, every crack, every chip.

LEO: Six years old, I was six years old, I remember, when I sat on this window seat and watched Granny drag Oupa to church. The Sunday after VE Day…

LULU: Are the cars all ready for the off?

LEKO: Make sure, Khokoloho.

KHOKO: (*In a strangled voice.*) I did. I did already.

LEKO: What's the matter?

KHOKO: Just had a drink of water and I think I swallowed a gogga.

NYATSO giggles. Suddenly DIKELEDI marches up to him and slaps NYATSO's face hard. Then marches back to near the door and just looks proudly at him.

KARLOTTA: Bakgat! *[i.e.: Afrikaans: Great stuff!]*

She applauds. General amazement and merriment; ANNA and MARIA hug her. Exit NYATSO.

LULU: After we've gone there won't be a soul left here.

LEKO: Not counting my boys.

LULU: Of course…

MARIA has found PUTSWA's stick behind a tea chest; brandishes it.

MARIA: Look! Putswa left his stick. (*LEKO pretends to cower.*) What's the matter with you? Oh, honestly, Mr Lebaka, the thought never even crossed…

She sticks it in the riempies of the window seat. PITSO makes like a megaphone.

PITSO: Ladies and gents, flight one-oh-four is about to depart!

MARIA: Look, Pitso, here's your vrot old cap!

Lying under the window seat, a baseball cap with the SA flag logo; she tosses it to PITSO, who catches it.

PITSO: My life is complete.

LEO notices the old teddy bear in the tea chest, rescues it and then props it up on the window seat.

LULU: We're off. Let's go.

She collects her coat from DIKELEDI and kisses her goodbye. Exit MARIA, KARLOTTA, NYATSO, KELE severally. A moment's pause. LEKO is jingling the house keys.

LEKO: Nobody left behind? There's are files and stuff in there – must lock up.

House keys in one hand, he makes for ANNA's door. She leaps to bar his way.

ANNA: NO!

LEKO: (*Backing off.*) OK, OK…

ANNA: Totsiens to you, house. Totsiens the old life.

PITSO: And viva to the new! (*He holds out his hand to her.*)

Exit PITSO and ANNA hand in hand. A pause. LEKO, jingling his keys impatiently, crosses to the door, stops near LULU. She holds his gaze for a moment.

LULU: Leko. I think it's thank you.

They clasp hands for a moment. Then Exit LEKO.

KHOKOLOHO Enters to close the shutters and swings the bar down to lock them. The room darkens; brilliant bars of sunlight cut through the slats on to the floor. Exit KHOKOLOHO, chuckling to himself.

LULU and LEO sit together on the window-seat, like small children, holding hands. The teddy bear sits next to them.

LULU: Mama so loved to read in here…

O/S ANNA and PITSO's voices call together: 'Mummy/Looloo.'

LULU: (*Calling back.*) Ye-es! (*She gets up.*)

LEO: (*sobbing like a kid.*) Luly, Luly…

O/S: again the two voices calling.

LULU: Goodbye, Mama… (*She calls back.*) Coming, coming children…!

She takes LEO's hand and leads him out of the room. Two cars start up and drive off into the distance. Then a third. Silence. A shuffle of feet from behind the empty bookcases.

Enter PUTSWA very slowly, chuntering to himself. He takes in the empty room. He attempts to lift the heavy bar on the shutters, but is too weak to manage. He sits on the window seat, very still. He finds his stick left upright in the riempies and leans his old head on it.

Suddenly the chainsaws start their whine, first one and then another and another. The crack of falling trees. A crescendo of sound until the volume is unbearable. Then utter silence.

The lights fade on PUTSWA, sitting silent.

End.

Glossary

Words and expressions are listed in the order they appear in the play. Afk means Afrikaans in origin.

Ek is jou Pappie se spook – (Afk): I am your Daddy's ghost – a send-up version of 'I am your father's spirit' – *Hamlet* Act 1, Scene 7.

Hé la/hé lang – (Sotho): singular and plural exclamation of surprise, disbelief or dissaproval; also an expression of fellow-feeling in conversation; also meaning well, or I say at the beginning of a speech. Accents indicate pronunciation only.

U nkentse letswalo – (Sotho): Literally, you've put bad luck into me; brought me…

Mampara – (affectionately): an idiot, a fool.

Awa – (Sotho): no.

Moshomane – (Sotho): singular, boy. Bashimane, plural.

Mosetsane – (Sotho): singular, girl. Mosetsana u stout = naughty girl. Stout: a borrowed Afk word widely used by Sotho speakers.

BiMa 7 – slang: BMW 7 series.

Wa-ikgantsha – (Sotho): show-off; boast.

Ishu! – (S.Sotho): ouch! or an exclamation expressing a variety of emotions, especially surprise, wonder, or relief.

Dumela/dumelang – (Sotho): singular and plural of a greeting – good day, good morning.

Baas – boss, sir, master, employer, manager, supervisor; used of or to a white male to indicate the speaker's perception or acknowledgment of the other's superior status – now offensive and often used ironically.

Nê – (Afk colloquial): an interrogative particle, not so?; also used redundantly for emphasis.

Takkie – noun, colloquial: plimsoll, gym shoe.

Vrot – (Afk): rotten, no good, useless.

Loop – (Afk): run along, go, off with you.

Ouk (or ou) – noun colloquial: type, bloke, character, ordinary citizen, mate; a person. Can be used for male or female.

Parathlathlé – (Sotho): 'Disaster City' is an acceptable approximation. In the original Twenty-two Misfortunes is a rough translation of the Russian. In the InGuni languages 'th' is not pronounced as in the English 'the', but the 'h' is silent as if it were 'Paratlatlé'.

Doek – (Afk): head-scarf.

Jy weet – (Afk): You know.

Sommer so – (Afk): simply, just, for no specific reason, without more ado.

Pietertjie – (Afk): also Antjie, Marietjie – the affectionate diminutive to any noun in Afk is achieved by the addition of the suffix tjie. Pronounced k.

Now-now – colloquial: instantly, also when I feel like it.

Skattie – (Afk): a term of endearment, like little darling or treasure.

Oos wes tuis bes – (Afk): east, west, home is best.

Snoep – colloquial: mean, tight-fisted.

Idées au-dessus de son gare – joke Franglais for ideas above his station. *Gare* means railway station in French.

Klap – (Afk): clout, hit, strike, whack.

Vrot – (Afk): rotten, spoiled, worn out.

Lekker – (Afk): nice, pleasant, good, lovely. Initially used only of food and drink, but subsequently broadened in usage.

Cherrie – colloquial: chick, girlfriend, girl, virgin.

Mosadinayana – (Sotho): white woman, madam.

Wena – (Sotho/Zulu): you.

Ek sê – colloquial: from Afk I say, or I'm telling you; an exclamation used to attract attention or as an entry into a remark or conversation.

Yes-no – from Afk ja-nee, as in Is wine an aphrodisiac? Yes – no, it depends.

Gauleiter – (German): German officer.

Kea leboha – (Sotho): thank you very much.

Sister – a courteous term of address or reference to a woman; or an accolade meaning, in the political sense, a sister in the struggle, a comrade. Brother or bra' has the same weight of meaning.

MBA – (degree course): Master of Business Administration.

Gogo – (Zulu): a term of respect for an elderly person; also used generally as a title, i.e. granny.

Affirmative action – policy of promoting black people in preference to whites in the interests of black empowerment.

Melktert – (Afk): a traditional baked custard tart flavoured with spice.

De Beers – international diamond-selling consortium.

Ficksburg – small town in the eastern Free State on the Lesotho border famous for its annual cherry festival. The Free State grows ninety per cent of the cherry crop in SA.

Vaal Dam – a popular water-sports venue, south of Johannesburg.

Amandhla! – (Xhosa/Zulu): power, strength; the rallying cry used by the ANC, which elicits the response ngawethu! Meaning Is ours!

Bayette – (Zulu): hail! – the Zulu royal salute; also extended as an honour to prominent persons or high officials.

Pik – (Afk) Pickett's nickname meaning little fellow, small child, probably from piccanin; also any small object. Equivalent to tiny in English when applied to a very tall man. Used either affectionately or with contempt.

Die liewe – (Afk): dear.

Skande – (Afk): shame, scandal.

Pas op – (Afk): watch it, take care, look out. Also inverted as *Opass.*

Sala hantle – (Sotho): stay in peace, stay well, goodbye.

Meneer – (Afk): Mr, sir.

Gerrie – (Afk): diminutive form of the boy's name Gerrit. Pronounced g as in loch.

Neewat – (Afk): colloquial – literally no what; in this case an expression of dismay.

Rooibos – a herbal tea much beloved of health-minded South Africans, and indeed world-wide.

Outa – (Afk): literally old father – an elderly black man.

Poulêt de luxe – Franglais pun on luxuriously scented *poulets* (chickens), and poules (prostitutes).

Dutchman – (slang): a derogatory and offensive name for an Afrikaner; used affectionately here. Both upper and lower case can be used.

Verligte – (Afk): progressive, open-minded.

Court of Appeal – Bloemfontein is the judicial capitl of SA and the highest court in the land sits there.

The horns of the ox – Shaka, King of the Zulus was a daring military strategist and devised a fearsome frontal attack (the 'chest') and two curving laterals (the 'horns'), with another battalion ('the loins') kept in reserve.

Wragtig! – (Afk): really, for real, truly.

Shesha – (Zulu colloquial): hurry up, step on it. Pronounced tshetsha.

Lekker slaap – (Afk): sleep well, happy dreams.

Schloep, also shloop – (onomatopoeic slang): suck up to, toady, sweet-talk, ingratiate oneself.

Shmooze – as above.

Puthu, or putu – (Zulu colloquial): maize-meal porridge; a staple diet.

Solnyshko mayó, moy vesényi tsvetóchek – Russian: My
little sunshine, my spring flower. In Chekhov's original
play. (Accents for emphasis only)

ACT TWO

Imbira – a traditional hand-held instrument; a wooden
sounding-board on which differing lengths of metal are
struck with the thumbs.

Doring boom – (Afk): thorn tree.

Blerrie or blerry – bloody; this orthography is generally
used to represent the pronunciation of Afrikaans
speakers.

Foeitog – (Afk): an exclamation expressing disapproval,
distress, sympathy, pity; sometimes used ironically.
From Afk foei (for shame) + tog (all the same).

Die arme diertjies – (Afk): the poor little animals.

Kleintjies – (Afk): little children.

Niemand – (Afk): no one.

Sarie Marais – (Afk): popular love song.

> Oh my Sarie Marais is so far from my heart
>
> I hope to see her again
>
> Over there in the cornfields by the old thorn tree
>
> There lives my Sarie Marais.
>
> *Refrain*
>
> Oh take me back to the old Transvaal
>
> There's where my Sarie lives…

Verskriklik – (Afk): frightening, terrible, shocking.

Hou jou bek, jong – (Afk): shut your mouth, young man; zip
it, shut up.

Vat jou goed en trek Ferreira – (Afk): Boer War folk song:

> Take your things and leave, Ferreira
>
> Johnnie with the crippled leg… (repeated)

Ons sing net soos 'n jakals – (Afk): We sing just like a jackal.

Slim Jannie – (Afk): clever clogs, smartass.

Heeltemaal alleen – (Afk): completely alone.

Baboon Spider – (probably translated South African Dutch: baviaan spinnekop) any of several large, hairy, burrowing spiders of the Theraphosidae.

Gogga – (Afk): collective term for creeping and slithering creatures; insect.

Trop gentil – (French): too kind.

Portugoose – colloquial pronunciation for Portuguese; used affectionately, or not.

Tu peux t'en aller – (French): you may go.

'Klippie' – (Afk): nickname meaning stony, hard, rock-like.

Sethoto – (Sotho): stupid.

Skollies – (colloquial): young thug, rascal, street hoodlum, rogue; especially in the Cape: a Coloured gang member.

Ntate – (Sotho): father, polite form of address to an older man.

Ngunu – (Sotho): grandfather, as above.

Ramaphosa, Cyril R. – a trade unionist and former Secretary General of the ANC, in line for elevation in Mandela's government but stepped down to concentrate on business interests; has emerged as the standard-bearer of black economic empowerment and was arguably SA's most influential black businessman.

uBuntu – (Zulu colloquial): – the qualities embodying the values and virtues of essential humanity; or of Africanness. A very Mandelian attribute.

Kaffir – (from Arabic kafir; infidel): an insulting and contemptuous term for a black African, or occasionally for any black person.

The children of '76 – refers to the schoolchildren of Soweto who bravely instigated marches against the use of Afrikaans as a medium of instruction in black schools; possibly the first children's revolution in history.

'Die Stem van Suid Afrika' – (Afk): the Call of South Africa – the former national anthem, retained after the democratic elections alongside the black African hymn of freedom 'Nkosi sikelel i Afrika' as joint anthems of the new South Africa.

Poetical translation

> Ringing out from our blue heavens
>
> From our deep seas breaking round
>
> Over everlasting mountains
>
> Where the echoing crags resound…

Eskies asseblief meneer, is ek op pad na die stasie? – (Afk): Excuse me please, sir, am I on the right road for the station?

Bethlehem – to the east, and the town of Virginia to the west, are the two nearest main-line train stations in the area.

Hotnot – (colloquial): an insulting term of address to a Coloured (mixed race) person. From Hottentot, a native tribe of the Cape.

Kleinmiesies – (Afk colloquial): little miss, little madam.

Sal die kleinmiesies iets vir my gee? – (Afk): will the little madam give me something?

Voetsak! – (colloquial): fuck off, bugger off, go away, get out of it.

Asseblieftog – (Afk): I beg you, please.

Dronkie – (Afk colloquial): drunkard, wino, derelict.

Still thinks it's against the law – refers to the Immorality Act, rescinded in 1985, which banned sexual relationships between people of different race.

Madiba – affectionate name for Mandela; his clan name.

Deurmekaar – (Afk): confused, muddled, disorganised, bohemian.

Verneuk – (Afk): fool, deceive, trick, swindle.

Skellum – (Afk): rascal, rogue, scoundrel; also used affectionately.

ACT THREE

Niks nie – (Afk): nothing.

Bakgat – (Afk): good, excellent, fine, pleasing.

Hy's 'n goeie mens 'n slegte musikant – (Afk): he's a good man but a bad musician. In Chekhov's original play, in German: *Guter Mensch aber schlechter Musikant.*

Aandag assebleif – (Afk): attention please.

Dames en here – (Afk): ladies and gentlemen.

Bonsewer monsewer – (French): *bonsoir monsieur,* badly pronounced.

Tsotsis – (origin unknown; perhaps a Sotho corruption of zoot suit): used affectionately or contemptuously, a bad young man; gangster, hoodlum.

Laanie – (colloquial, origin unknown): a noun derogatory – 1a: a white man, boss, employer; 2a: a member of the upper classes; B adjective: posh, elegant, smart. Often used derogatorily by black speakers.

Hayi suka – in the Nguni languages it can be used as an interjection to mean surprise, disbelief, reproof, disgust; as in get away!, I don't believe you, go on.

Hamba! – (Zulu): go!, get out of it! Widely used all over SA.

Kaalvoet – (Afk): barefoot.

Bashimane – (Sotho): boys. Singular = mashimane.

Pondoks – (Afk from Malay): a rough shelter, hut, or shanty; loosely (often jokingly) a small house.

Shosholoza

> *Shosholoza, sithwele kanzima, sithwele kanzima*
> *(Ooh, aah!) [repeat x8]*
> *Etshe shosholoza!*

> *Chorus*
> *Shosholoza kulezontaba*
> *Stimela si ohaamuka e South Africa*
> *Stimela si ohamuka e South Africa*

Wena u ya baleka, wena u ya baleka
Kulezontaba
Stimela si ohamuka e South Africa

The English meaning of this song roughly translates as:

Push, push, pushing on and on
There's much to be done
Push, push, pushing in the sun
We will push as one

Work, work, working in the sun
We will work as one
Work, work, working in the rain
Til there's sun again.

Amongst black South Africans communal singing was traditionally in the a capella style, without instrumental accompaniment. Indigenous music for groups contained at least two vocal parts – one for the leader and one for the chorus. These songs were sung en masse at important events such as weddings, funerals, births, preparation for battle, hunting and so on.

When European missionaries began to convert Africans to Christianity during the 1800s, a new form of choral singing developed amongst the converts. This style combined some of the rules of European classical music and hymnody with the indigenous choral mode. The term which describes this hybrid form is 'makwaya', 'kwaya' being a phonetically-spelt version of 'choir'.

African labourers usually sing or chant to provide a work-rhythm and to ease the co-ordination of heavy work. Shosholoza apparently originated amongst railway gangers, since both the words and the rhythms suggest the movement of a piston-driven train. The song later began to be used as a protest song, and an emblematic revolutionary song of triumph over white oppression.

Bhari – (Sotho): meaning slow-witted, applied to country folk.

Net een botteltjie vir die tjaffer – (Afk): just one little bottle for the kaffir; he is ironically quoting the white barman. Spelling denotes pronunciation.

Santé – (French): a toast: your good health.

Fort Hare – The University College of Fort Hare in the eastern Cape. To quote from Mandela's autobiography *Long Walk to Freedom*: 'Until 1960… Fort Hare… was the only residential centre of higher education for blacks in SA… it was a beacon for African scholars from all over Southern, Central and Eastern Africa. For young black South Africans like myself, it was Oxford and Cambridge, Harvard and Yale all rolled into one.'

Wits – affectionate nickname for the University of the Witwatersrand, Johannesburg.

Witboetie – ironic inversion of kaffirboetie (i.e. brother to a kaffir): abusive reference to a black friendly with whites.

RDP – the Reconstruction and Development Programme of the ANC movement.

Viva – (probably from Portugese): used as a salute at left-wing political rallies; here used ironically.

Eya – (Sotho): yes.

Tsamaya – (Sotho): go. Tsamaya sentle = go well.

Kwa-Masophaville – in the Nguni languages, at the place of; the prefix kwa is used to form place names as in Kwa-Zulu.

Shapka – (Russian): (fur) hat.

Toyi-toyi – (originally source unknown): a quasi-military double-time marching step performed by participants in protest marches and gatherings, accompanied by chanting, singing and shouting of slogans.

My baasie – my baas is usually more deferential than baas; with 'ie' (the diminutive) added it becomes an ironic term of address.

The great man – refers to Barney Simon, founder and artistic director of the Market Theatre, Johannesburg, until his untimely death in '95. In accepting the prestigious Jujamcyn Award on behalf of the theatre he said: 'Freedom through legislation has come suddenly and swiftly, and that is cause for great celebration. But freedom of the heart and mind is lagging far behind. It is *that* freedom that has always been our concern, and remains it. We know that for a time we will continue to live in contradiction and confusion.'

Alles sal regkom – (Afk): literally, everything will come right; all's well that ends well.

C'est tellement chèr – (French): it's so expensive.

'Jan Pierewiet' – an Afk folk song:
Jan Pierewiet, Jan Pierewiet, Jan Pierewiet staan stil (x2)
Goeie more my vrou, daars 'n soentjie vir jou
Goeie more my man, daar is Koffie in die kan.

Translation
J.P. stand still/ Good morning my wife, here's a kiss for you/
Good morning my husband, there's coffee in the pot.

Jou mammie gaan weg my kleintjie, totsiens my skatterbol – (Afk): your mummy's going away my little one, goodbye, my treasure.

My poppie, my liewe seuntjie moet nou gaan slaap – (Afk): – my dolly, my beloved little son, must go to sleep now.

Geagte – (Afk): honourable, honoured sir.

Molly-B – nickname for molybdenum (Mo), a chemical element used to impart superior strength to steel and other alloys at high temperature.

Allons-y – (French): let's go.

Muizenberg – a once fashionable coastal resort on the Indian ocean side of the Cape Peninsula.

Riempies – (Afk): thin strips of worked leather used especially for thonging the seats of chairs, settles, etc.

Chronology

1652	Jan van Riebeeck lands at the Cape of Good Hope, to establish the first European settlement.
1899-1902	Anglo-Boer War.
1910	Union of South Africa formed from the former Boer republics of Transvaal and Orange Free State, and the British colonies of the Cape and Natal.
1912	SA Native National Congress formed, later renamed the African National Congress (ANC)
1914	National Party formed.
1918	Nelson Mandela born.
1936	F.W. de Klerk born.
1948	National Party ousts General Smut's United Party and comes to power.
1950	SA Communist Party banned.
1955	Congress of the People adopts the Freedom Charter.
1958	Hendrik Verwoerd becomes prime minister.
1960	Sharpville massacre; ANC banned.
1961	SA declares itself a republic; leaves the Commonwealth.
1962	Mandela arrested, given five-year sentence.
1963	Police raid headquarters of Umkhonto we Sizwe (The Spear of the Nation) at Rivonia farm, arrest many ANC leaders.
1964	Mandela sentenced to life imprisonment.
1966	Verwoerd assassinated; John Vorster replaces him.
1976	Soweto revolt (the 'children's revolution').

1977	Death of black consciousness leader Steve Biko.
1978	P.W. Botha becomes Prime Minister, later President.
1979	Black trade unions legalised.
1982	Right-wing whites break away to form Conservative Party.
1983	New tri-cameral Constitution denies power to blacks; United Democratic Front formed to fight it.
1984-6	Township uprising; states of emergency declared ('85 and '86)
1985	
August	The Rubicon débâcle and the unilateral debt moratorium.
November	Nelson Mandela and Kobie Coetzee begin secret meetings.
1986	Thabo Mbeki and Pieter de Lange meet secretly in New York; National Party holds crucial Federal Congress.
1987	Mells Park House talks begin.
1988	Neil Barnard team begins meeting Mandela in prison.
1989	
February	F.W. de Klerk elected NP leader after P.W. Botha suffers stroke.
July	Botha and Mandela meet at Tuynhuys.
September	De Klerk elected President, legalises ANC Capetown march.
October	Walter Sisulu and ANC leaders released from prison.
December	De Klerk meets Mandela.

1990

February	De Kelk legalises ANC and SACP, and releases Mandela.
May	Talks begin at Groote Schuur estate in Capetown.
August	ANC suspends armed struggle; violence escalates.

1991

January	Nelson Mandela and Chief Mangosutho Buthelezi meet.
July	ANC holds key policy conference in Durban.
December	Start of formal multi-party talks, the Convention for a Democratic South Africa (Codesa 1).

1992

March	Whites-only referendum endorses reform.
May	Codesa 11 collapses.
June	ANC supporters killed at Boipatong.
September	Bisho massacre, followed by conclusion of the Record of Understanding between the ANC and Government.
October	Joe Slovo publishes article offering 'sunset clauses'.

1993

April	Chris Hani assassinated.
July	Agreement on election date, Inkatha walks out.
August	Mandela secretly meets Constand Viljoen of Conservatives.
November	Agreement on interim constitution.
December	Transitional Executive Council, the multi-party interim government begins to operate.

1994

March · Overthrow of Bophutaswana, rout of the white right.

April · Inkatha enters elections.

APRIL 26-8: · ANC WINS SOUTH AFRICA'S FIRST DEMOCRATIC ELECTION.

May · Mandela inaugurated, government of national unity formed.

1995

June · SA wins Rugby World Cup on home turf.

1996

May · New Constitution adopted, to take force in 1999.

June · National Party withdraws from GNU.

1999

June · The second democratic elections. Thabo Mbeki is inaugurated as the new President, after Nelson Mandela retires, after one term of office. The Democratic Party emerges as the new official but very small opposition. Thabo Mbeki is eventually ousted by Jacob Zuma who is currently President.

The Story unfolds...

Janet Suzman was born in Johannesburg, graduated from the University of the Witwatersrand, trained at LAMDA, and joined the RSC for its inaugural quatercentenary season, the Wars of the Roses in 1962 playing Joan la Pucelle. She stayed on and off in Stratford and London for a decade playing many of the heroines and culminating in a memorable Cleopatra in 1973. She has since pursued a richly varied career in all manner of performance disciplines; among them, *The Singing Detective* on TV and *The Draughtsman's Contract* on film, and her favourite, Fellini's *And The Boat Sails On.* She has twice won *The Evening Standard* Best Actress Award (Chekhov's *Three Sisters* and Fugard's *Hello and Goodbye*), had Academy Award and Golden Globe nominations (*Nicholas and Alexandra*), twice won The *Liverpool Echo* Best Production Award (Miller's *Death of a Salesman* and Shakespeare's *Antony and Cleopatra*), and also the TMA Best Production for her production of *The Cherry Orchard* at Birmingham Repertory Theatre in 1997. *The Johannesburg Othello* - so named by Channel Four TV and aired in 1987 – was her directorial debut for The Market Theatre, of which she is a founding Patron. She re-wrote and directed Brecht's *Good Woman of Setzuan,* renamed *The Good Person of Sharkville* changing it to a Johannesberg slum setting. She has written a handbook on playing with blank verse: *Acting with Shakespeare – The Comedies published by* Applause Books, NY.

She was appointed DBE for services to drama in 2011.